THE RUSTIC SCRIBE

Also by R. W. F. Poole

HUNTING: AN INTRODUCTION
A BACKWOODSMAN'S YEAR

THE RUSTIC SCRIBE

R. W. F. Poole

illustrations by Reginald Bass

Michael Joseph
LONDON

MICHAEL JOSEPH LTD

Published by the Penguin Group
Penguin Books Ltd, 27 Wrights Lane, London W8 5TZ, England
Viking Penguin, a division of Penguin Books USA Inc.,
375 Hudson Street, New York, New York 10014, USA
Penguin Books Australia Ltd, Ringwood, Victoria, Australia
Penguin Books Canada Ltd, 2801 John Street, Markham, Ontario, Canada L3R 1B4
Penguin Books (NZ) Ltd, 182–190 Wairau Road, Auckland 10, New Zealand

Penguin Books Ltd, Registered Offices: Harmondsworth, Middlesex, England

First published in Great Britain 1991

Printed in England by Clays Ltd, St Ives plc
Filmset in 11½/12½ pt Monophoto Palatino

A CIP catalogue record for this book is available from the British Library
ISBN 0 7181 3337 4

The moral right of the author has been asserted

CONTENTS

INTRODUCTION

There is a certain question that I have learnt to expect and which crops up wherever I go: 'How did you become a writer?' It is usually obvious that the questioners are perplexed. The little bubbles rise out of their heads and it is easy to see what they contain . . .

Thinks: 'How did this great red-faced hulk of a creature with arms like a navvy and hands like shovels ever come to pick up a pen? How has it come about that a man whose life (by his own account) has revolved around foxes, hounds, sheep and whisky should be writing books and having his work appear regularly in well-known magazines and the top national broadsheet? This creature is nothing like what a writer ought to be. I mean, you know, it did not really ought to be allowed.'

My answer to the spoken question is usually, 'Well, I just fell into it really.' This seems to quieten questioners, but does not answer them. As to the *Thinks*, I can only say that it is as great a source of wonderment to me as it obviously is to them.

Perhaps it would be no bad thing to dig a little deeper into my past and see if we can come up with a better explanation.

I have always devoured books, very often three at a time and if you do not understand how that can be done, then you are not a reader. I love words. They roll round my head in the same way that wine rolls round the mouth, releasing delicious tastes and fragrances. The Good Lord has granted me a facility in transferring these words to paper.

A facility needs training and discipline.

Miss James taught at my preparatory school. She was tiny, incandescent and Welsh. With her you learnt to write clear, simple, grammatical English; or Heaven help you, Butty Bach.

At Eton I developed a taste for hunting and brightly coloured socks. Mr M. A. Nicholson, my long suffering Classical Tutor, used to wince at both and then encourage me in my reading and writing. He even said I might consider Journalism as a career.

Some twenty years later I had my first article published by Mr Michael Clayton in *Horse and Hound*. I am deeply grateful to him.

The Arthur James column in *Shooting Times* started in the early eighties. Three editors later it is still running, although no one quite knows why.

In May 1987 I gave up hunting hounds after twenty-one years. It was a difficult moment. It would have been a lot more difficult but for the fact that my first *Daily Telegraph* article appeared in the same month. I thought that this was a great privilege for an unknown scribbler and I still do. I shall always be grateful to Max Hastings and Trevor Grove for giving me such a chance. You must ask them for the why of it.

The pieces in this book all appeared in the *Daily Telegraph*, *Sunday Telegraph* and *Telegraph* magazine between May 1987 and the end of 1989. It will be quite obvious that some of them are anachronistic, but that must be inevitable in a collection of journalistic gobbets.

As to myself, I still live in Northumberland and rejoice in my view. I am still married. I am no longer a Master of Foxhounds. I still have my sheep, but instead of being a farmer who writes, I am now a writer who farms. How did I become a writer? Well, I just fell into it really.

Northumberland,
January 1990

Chapter One

THE
LIFE AND TIMES
OF A RUSTIC SCRIBE

I SUPPOSE THAT I was a victim of my environment. My great uncle hunted his own hounds for forty seasons. My grandfather was a Master of Hounds. My father would have liked to have been one. He had two 78 records with the sounds of the chase on them and used to play them every morning whilst shaving. The cry of hounds and the musical voice of one of the great huntsmen of England were early imprints on my infant subconscious.

I was bred and buttered in Cornwall. My father was away at the war, and my mother and I lived with my grandmother.

Torfrey is a hideous granite house which looks out over the Fowey River. For a small boy it was paradise. The unkempt grounds, the home farm, and all the surrounding wild countryside were mine to wander at will.

After the war, Father went to work in London, and we moved to Surrey. I can still remember how horrified I was by blameless suburbia. I missed *my* river, and *my* woods, and I missed the curlew. That has been my measure ever since: I do not want to live anywhere where the curlews do not come.

Hunting played no part in my life at this time. There had been no hunting in our part of Cornwall during the war, and it certainly was not on the local menu at Virginia Water. But I suppose that the genes were in there somewhere, polishing their little boots, hissing through their teeth, and waiting for the moment to assert themselves. It came at Eton.

My schooldays were uniformly dreary. I shone neither academically nor socially. I learnt to love books and solitude.

Then I discovered Hounds. The Eton College Beagles are the oldest school pack. Over the years they have turned out many famous masters of hounds, some not so famous, some disasters; and me. Hunting became the passion of my life. I devoured every book on the subject that I could stick my grimy thumb in. I actually rose to the dizzy heights of Second Whipper-in to the Beagles, but I always regarded beagling as a stepping stone to higher things; after all, running is a pretty moderate form of getting about and lacks glamour, especially when I do it. I wanted the glamour, the dash, the hurroosh, of foxhunting. It is possible that I might have been also influenced by pictures that sometimes appeared in the glossy magazines of shiny-booted masters of foxhounds who always seemed to be festooned with beautiful and adoring women. It seemed to me that that would be the best possible cure for the acne to which I was a martyr at the time.

The chances of becoming a MFH seemed remote. I had no money (as my father pointed out) and no apparent ability (as everybody pointed out). Human nature is a very peculiar thing. Sometimes when the pipe is drawing nicely I do wonder whether I would have become quite so determined to hunt hounds if so many kind people had not spent so much time explaining why it was impossible.

The next move was to a Dickensian office in the City where I was articled to a chartered accountant. Father was mesmerized by chartered accountancy (not being one himself): I felt as though I had been chucked into the slammer. I served four years' penal servitude in the City, but there were moments of remission. The Bisley and Sandhurst Foxhounds lived in the dripping conifers behind the Staff College at Camberley, and the hunt staff were very kind to me. They let me spend my spare time working in the kennels; they taught me to skin the fallen stock that was brought in to feed the hounds; they allowed me to be with the foxhounds. They even allowed me to put a caravan behind the slaughter-house so that I could move out of Kensington, be a commuter, and come home to my hounds every night.

I got my first terrier, Chipper, who shared the caravan with me and kept the rats at bay. I moved into the caravan in the autumn of 1962, nicely in time for the winter of 1962/63. I had also started growing a moustache; every morning it would be frozen solid. The caravan offered a choice of pneumonia or carbon monoxide poisoning, and was not conducive to studying accountancy (foxhunting was a much more interesting subject anyway). At last the Institute of Chartered Accountants refused to let me fail the intermediate exam any more. My long suffering employer (there were a lot of minor infections that coincided with hunting days) heaved a sigh of profound relief and bounced me.

On the first of May 1964 I became Master and Huntsman of the Dartmoor Foxhounds. The hunt gave me the princely sum of two thousand pounds out of which I had to pay all the expenses of the hunt and keep myself. I paid the Kennel Huntsman eight pounds a week, and myself five. We hunted three days a week and I learnt to skin and cut up a dead ewe for the pot in three minutes.

My first six months as MFH were disastrous. Everything that could, and several things that could not, went wrong. I resigned the night before my first opening meet. There then appeared two remarkable ladies to whom I owe an immense debt of gratitude. I called them 'the Missus' and 'Auntie Vi'. Between them (squabbling as they did so), they picked me up, wiped my nose, kicked my bum, bullied me, fed me, and cajoled me. It is thanks to them that I survived as a Master.

Dartmoor is a place that you either love or hate: I loved it. The hunting was wild and fast, and I thrived in the wild deeps of the moor.

There were two problems, however: the finance and the feuding. Every hunt committee is convinced that the Master spends all the hard-raised cash on booze and broads, and anyway feels that the bloody feller should be paying them for the honour of being Master. Thus finance can be a running, and sometimes bloody, skirmish. There are also some parts of the country where feuds are endemic and pursued with a primitive relish. On Dartmoor, one side of the moor has always fought the other, for no very good reason that anybody can remember. They might call a truce for a tempting target like a young, pink MFH, whom both sides could then stonk in turn.

In pursuit of a slightly quieter life and fiscal reality, I moved my few belongings and many terriers to the Wilton. The Wilton was, and I hope is, a happy country. As far as hunting went, the followers were like the forty-year-old virgin — thankful for small mercies. It was a country of big woodlands and chalk downs, where pheasants took priority over foxes. But it was fun. I was happy there, and if hunting on the good scenting hills of Dartmoor was like painting with a broad brush, to catch foxes on the cold chalk of Wiltshire required very fine and detailed brushwork. It was immensely valuable experience.

After four years there, the financial problems once more became insuperable, and on the first of May 1971 I awoke as an ex-MFH and wondered, what next?

I drove lorries. There was an interesting trip when I got stranded at Le Havre in the middle of a dock strike with four polo ponies, the wrong documentation, and a communist customs officer. The story includes a rescue by the local mayor and a sojourn in a hotel that was not quite what it seemed; but I will not bore you with that.

There was then a spell as a deckhand on a Panamanian coaster that took sand to Libya. I am afraid that no one else believes it, either.

A week before Christmas I walked into the kitchen of a friend's house and saw a girl. We were married in April. My wife had two MsFH in her family, and she had had enough of them. She wanted to marry a stockbroker, or anything other than a MFH; even a lorry driver. After a couple of months, however, she decided that unless I took another pack of hounds we would both be candidates for the funny farm.

In 1973 I took the Taunton Vale. My step-father-in-law looked at me over his spectacles and said that I would not like it, and would not stay there. Three years later he said that he had told me so, but that I would love the Sinnington. As usual, he was right.

If you were to attempt to express packs of hounds in

footballing terms, the Sinnington would have been in the top quarter of Division One. It was ruled by the Countess of Feversham, one of the greatest lady foxhunters of our times, whose Joint Master I became. Then began one of the happiest periods of my career, a time when I feel I reached the peak of whatever hunting skills I may lay claim to.

The Sinnington country lies in North Yorkshire. It is an old-fashioned and unspoilt country inhabited by old-fashioned and unspoilt people. It also has the biggest and strongest foxes in all England. I have no doubt that I had the best hunting of my life there.

A 'point' in hunting is the longest distance in a straight line that can be measured in the course taken by a hunted fox. These days, in most hunting countries, a four-mile point is regarded as unusual, and a hunt of ten miles as the fox runs, spectacular. My Sinnington diaries show points of ten, nine and eight miles, and many hunts of more than twenty miles. I could still talk you through some of those hunts yard by yard but, oh dear, how you would be yawning then; even if you are not now.

I am a large man. In 1964 it was said that I was too big to make a huntsman; by 1980 I was riding some 18 stone. In 1964, a quality heavyweight hunter could be bought for £300; by 1980 the price tag was £3000 and rising. Most of my life I have ridden not very good horses. Bad horses ridden across country by a bad horseman tend to have bad falls, which can be rather wearing. I lost my nerve. You cannot hunt hounds in a hard riding country when the bottle has gone. So I resigned.

That should really have been the end of the story. An old friend telephoned me and asked why I did not consider going to the West Percy in Northumberland? There was no jumping on the Cheviots, he said, and you will never get close enough to the hounds to spoil them. I said that I thought it unlikely that the West Percy would want a has-been like me. They have now put up with me for six happy years. The West Percy may have regrets but I have none.

For five years I hunted hounds in the wild border hills and

loved it, but the worm of doubt was nibbling away. I knew that I was slowing up. I also knew that increased commitments outside hunting meant that I was not devoting as much time to my hounds as I had done in the past. I knew that there was a man in the wings who would make a better job of it, and should be given the chance. On 30 April 1987 I hung up my hunting horn after twenty-one seasons. Hunting a pack of hounds was a strong and heady draught. Hunting as a spectator is small beer, pleasant and refreshing though it may be.

So what do I look back on over those years and some two thousand days hunting? Long hours in the saddle in all winds and weather; long hours in the kennel and stable, where there is no time, and you work until the work is done; moments of fear, moments of despair, but most of all moments of great joy and exhilaration. Hunting has opened many doors for me, and most of them are still open. I have met many truly nice people and very few nasty ones. I have been privileged to live and work in some of the most lovely parts of England. Perhaps, best of all, I have been privileged to work with the Foxhound. I have never much cared for the social or administrative side of hunting; it is the hounds and the hunting of them that have made everything worthwhile. I loved my hounds deeply. We are still friends and pleased to see each other, but they are not *mine* anymore in the way they once were, and I know that my life will never be quite the same again.

I was surprised when I was asked to write this piece. I have found my life interesting, but I am not sure that others will find it so. I suppose that even a potted autobiography ought to have a dedication, so I dedicate this piece to the Fox and The Foxhound, and to my wife who understood.

Chapter Two

THE
CUMBERLAND BROWN
SHED

THE FIRST THING that I did when I bought my little farm in the Cheviot Hills was to put up the shed. I suppose to be strictly truthful I had the road put in first. The farm was literally a green field site (which as we all know is now properly referred to as a Zero Development Base) the land having been sold away from the original steading. The shed is a single-span General Purpose Shed constructed with steel girders and metal sheeting. It is 140 feet long by 60 feet wide and is probably one of the best and wisest investments I have ever made.

The shed was supposed to be finished in the November so that all the interior fittings could be finished in good time to house four hundred ewes on 1 January, but that autumn, the whole of England seemed in danger of sinking back into the mud. The shed was not started until October, in the mud. Every day I used to stand and despair, in the mud. Every time I rode over the hill coming home from hunting, I would look across the valley at the gaunt skeleton, and Oh the Joy when I saw that during one day the first roof sheets had gone on.

Shows up a bit, said the Rest of the Valley: going to paint it, are you? I assured the Rest of the Valley that I was going to cover it with naked ladies in lascivious poses and fluorescent paint. The Rest of the Valley cheered up no end.

Now the shed has become part of the landscape (Cumberland Brown, if you really want to know) and part of my life. The ewes come in on 1 January and stay in until they lamb in April. This has a two-fold effect of resting the ground and shielding the girls from the worst of the winter blasts.

I am usually in the shed soon after 0630. I like the peace and quiet of the early morning which disappears instantly at the first rattle of the feed bag. Peace returns progressively as the troughs are filled. From the end door of the shed I can see the main road below the hill. By 0700 the rush hour is on; I may see as many as six sets of lights at once; pace of life up here is quite frightening sometimes.

Hay is the next job. It is all there in the shed; no need to step outside. Now comes the Pot Ale Syrup (a by-product of whisky distilling) which is poured on the hay. The ewes love it and it puts tremendous udders on them.

It will be about daybreak by now. Dawn over the Cheviots is always worth a look, at whatever time of year, and my shed must have one of the finest views in England. Soon it is breakfast time and there is nothing like a couple of hours' work to fettle the gastric juices. The house being just across the yard, I can usually smell the bacon as I come out of the shed: does anybody know a better smell on a frosty morning? (Oh yes, we built a house as well, but after the shed: house the sheep before the wife, question of priorities.)

There are always jobs to be done in the shed. When I tire of word processing, I can go across and potter about and convince myself that I am working. Sometimes I lean on my prong and watch the sleet driving horizontally past the end of the shed. I think of the mud and slush outside, and look at the ewes chewing contentedly on their thick dry bed of straw. Then I think what a good investment the shed was. I get some good thoughts in my shed, as I hope you will find out.

Chapter Three

THE
WEATHER FORECAST

WHAT ON EARTH would we do in dear old Britain without our weather? It provides an absorbing, universal, and totally safe topic of conversation. Complete strangers can bind on about it to each other safe in the knowledge that no social or political corns are being trodden on. Neither the Class Struggle nor Trade Union intransigence can be blamed on the weather, or vice versa: not directly anyway. There can be little doubt that people are affected by climate. Hot-blooded Latins are just that, their temperament made mercurial by constant exposure to too much sun. The native of Aberdeen who regularly receives bracing easterly winds up his bypass tends to take a somewhat dourer attitude to life. The Protestant Work Ethic is a good way of keeping warm. Biting showers of sleet are an effective curb to excessive passion.

The native of Skibbereen is likely to have a different approach. If he can see the mountains then he knows that it is going to rain. If he cannot see the mountains then this is because the rain has already obscured them. Either way he knows that it is a guinea to a gooseberry that if he goes out he is going to aggravate his chronic mildew. Is it not better to hold his hour and have another? And if the Good Lord sends a fine day tomorrow, well then is that not time enough to get the work done – always supposing that there is nothing better to do?

In between these two, we have rather neutral sort of weather. A bit of wet, a bit of fine, nothing really too extreme: something to moan about, but really nothing to get terribly excited about, my dear chap. Is this not exactly representative of the mainstream British character?

My peripatetic existence has lead me through most English weather zones. I think I am right in saying that the rainfall in the West of England varies between 70 and 100 inches. No Cornishman would dream of going anywhere without a waterproof coat. ('Take your coat when the weather is fine, and please yourself when it is raining.') One of the merry things about Dartmoor is that you can be trolling along, having a little hum, and remarking to yourself on the clemency of the day; then ten minutes later you can find yourself totally enveloped in grey swirling mist. The thing to remember then is that every stream runs into a river, and every river runs to the sea. If you find yourself passing the Eddystone Lighthouse then you have gone too far.

In my innocence I used to take the West Country climate and its enervating softness as the norm, and anyway it was positively Mediterranean compared to the quite incredibly dismal miasmas of the Thames Valley. I used to suffer my twice-yearly colds, my annual losing bout with influenza, and semi-permanent inflammation of the sinuses (sini?).

Northumberland has banished them all. I suppose that it is the sort of climate where what does not sicken will fatten. The air is the strongest I have encountered anywhere, and it is basically a hard dry climate (rainfall c. 28 ins.). The prevailing westerly wind whips along the Irish Sea and then arrives in my lungs after about a hundred miles of heather. It is great stuff even if it does lift the fillings out of the teeth occasionally.

I submit that it is the British weather that makes the average Briton what he is: rather plodding, easy going, sometimes pretty bloody minded and occasionally unpredictable.

Hooray for the Great British weather. Long may it rain over us.

Chapter Four

URBANS AND
RUSTICS

THE HIKERS STOLE my milk. I admit that the evidence is circumstantial, but I ask you to consider it with me. The milk is brought to the end of the farm road. Our turbocharged milkman has neither the time nor the inclination to tackle our goat track. On this particular day, the milk was delivered but, when the despatch rider went down to collect it, it had disappeared. I held an immediate court of enquiry in the village. Ah, said the Village, shaking its head, it will have been the hikers. Three of them had come through the village during the time in question, bobbled of hat, and hairy of face and leg; with large rucksacks, quite capable of holding purloined milk bottles. Where is the proof? There is none; but such is the current rural suspicion of Urban Man that none was felt necessary.

We Rustics are starting to feel like a persecuted minority. We feel that we are under increasing threat from Urban Man. We feel that the Urbs are out to get us; to 'improve' us; to change our way of life, and to turn the places where we live, and work, into a Great Rural Theme Park, an extension of Clapham Common or Richmond Park. We Rustics are not over the moon at the prospect; I go so far as to say that we are sick as parrots about it.

To many of us, the hikers are the stormtroopers of this invasion. The shrill, propagandist rantings of the Ramblers' Association have an uncomfortably familiar tone; rather like that funny, little man with the tatty moustache who was always demanding *Lebensraum*. They want us to open up our homes to their brightly-hued members, as of right; they are certainly not concerned with winning our hearts and minds. My lawful occasions often take me into the hills, and I come upon a great number of hikers; I always greet them and attempt to pass the time of day. Some are very pleasant people, who feel, as I do, that one is nearer to God, in high silent places. Others are surly and, on occasion, downright unpleasant; whatever hiking may be doing for them, it certainly does not appear to be beneficial. Apart from ill manners, there is an element of malice amongst some of these people: stone walls pulled down, trees vandalized, and gates left open with, sometimes, disastrous results for livestock.

A friend of mine has a farm that bestrides a footpath to a well-known beauty spot. He happened to be out on his tractor one day when he spied a party of school children who were not on the path, by a long measure. He watched them go through a gate, between two carefully sorted lots of sheep, and leave the gate wide open. It will hardly surprise you when I tell you that he went across to the bearded wonder, who appeared to be in charge, to reason with him in a Christian spirit and to suggest that he and his should shut the gate. You may, or may not, be surprised that the teacher then addressed my friend as a 'F—— Peasant': it was a mistake. On the foreloader of the tractor was the gripe, which is a spiked bucket used for shifting muck. I do not suppose that the manufacturers had such a use in mind, but the gripe also comes in very useful for shifting loutish ushers across a field at high speed.

You may think that I do not welcome Urban Man in the country; this is not the case, but I do think that it is up to him to deserve his welcome, and not to expect it on demand.

Ramblers have become known as 'Plastic Pigs' or 'Fell Rats'; if they want more attractive descriptions then they have got to earn them – and they can start by leaving my milk alone.

Chapter Five

DOGS ARE A
TAUTOLOGY

I LIKE A BIT of droving. A fine morning, the pipe drawing
nicely; the horn heid stick, and the tackety boots, swinging
rythmically. With the sheep moving at a friendly pace, there
is time to look about, and to compliment the Almighty on his
handiwork, and the fact that the lines have fallen unto me in
pleasant places. Mind you, it is a different story on a stinker of
a morning, but then I would simply postpone the operation,
and write an article about it instead.

I do not do as much droving as I used to. At one time I had
sheep scattered about all over; in different fields, in different
places. Lorries are expensive, and the cheapest way to shuttle
sheep about, or to return them to base, is to make use of the
four legs with which thoughtful nature has provided them.

The best time for droving is the early morning. A four
o'clock start, on a fine summer's morning, is no hardship.
Everything is fresh and clean, and the sheep travel best in the
cool of the day. It also means that we can be through the
village, and its well tended flowerbeds, before the more tidy-
minded citizens are awake enough to call down the wrath of
the patron saint of gardeners on my head — although the
evidence of our passing will be there for them to tread in later
on.

The early hour also means less motor traffic. It is really a
great nuisance that people should want to drive along roads
which I require for the movement of my sheep; I cannot
encourage such irresponsible behaviour. In a moment of weak-
ness, I once took a drove of lambs into a field to let some cars

past. I had overlooked the fact that the field also contained a Pony Club rally. To the best of my knowledge and belief, none of those lambs was a member of the Pony Club, but they joined in the frolics with tremendous enthusiasm. It took me half an hour of hortative blasphemy to separate them from their new-found chums, and return them to the path of duty and the road. This experience had a profound effect on myself, and the members of the Pony Club who subsequently tried out the new words on their parents. I now harden my heart to all following traffic.

You may have got the impression that I am doing all this on my own. This is not so; there are the dogs, of course. You can do nothing with sheep without dogs. I have three: a highly-bred Scotsman with all the dour dedication of his race; a doubtfully bred Yorkshire bitch with a mind like a computer; and what is generally known as 'thatbloodyredAustralianb——'. This last is a Kelpie, an Australian sheepdog. If you have never seen one, they are small and red, with prick ears; they look a bit like a large fox. They have boundless enthusiasm and stamina, and they bark and bark and bark. They are great droving dogs. Sheep tend quickly to lose their initial enthusiasm for the outing; those in front want to stop and pick delicacies out of the hedge; if the front stops, then so does the back. Kelpies will have none of this frivolity. They go to the front, and bark at the leaders to keep them moving; they then come all the way back down the column, keeping each file on the move; round the end, then back up the column again. They will do this for hours at a stretch. The Scotsman mans the rearguard, and woe betide any sheep that tries to break back. The bitch provides the forethought. Once she has travelled a route, she seems to remember every bolt hole on the way. When one of these is coming up, she will disappear and the disappointed sheep will find her, in the gap, grinning hugely.

If you ever get stuck behind a fat man with a pipe and a drove of sheep, you should abandon all hope, and seek another route; my heart is set like concrete. I will offer you sympathy, but not passage. I dare not risk upsetting the Pony Club again.

Chapter Six

HARROGATE HOUND SHOW

To Harrogate Hound Show. Let us establish something at once: hound shows are for hounds, working foxhounds, beagles, harriers, etc. The canine world is divided into Hounds and Cur Dogs: your Crufts champion, madam, and your pedigree Labrador, sir, are Cur Dogs. I hope that you are all with me so far. Hound shows have two purposes. The first is to help people establish the correct physical shape for a hound since a well-designed hound will do more work, faster, than a badly-designed hound: QED. The second, and more important, purpose is to give hunting people the chance to meet and have a jolly, during the long summer months when there is no hunting to interrupt the tedium of work.

There are six main hound shows in Britain: Harrogate, Peterborough, Ardingly, Honiton, Rydal and Builth Wells. Most have a major agricultural show clinging to their coat tails; for instance, The Great Yorkshire Show happens somewhere on the outskirts of the Harrogate Hound Show.

Hounds are shown by their respective hunt servants, in full hunting livery (but no spurs), and judged by Very Senior Masters of Hounds. Hound judging is pretty esoteric, and it is enough to say that hounds are judged on their stamina points, their pace points, and their movement. They are also judged according to the personal prejudices of the judges, but you are not supposed to know that so please forget that I told you.

It is a colourful sight, the ring full of red coats (never, never Pink), white breeches and shining boots (the men), and lemon, black, mottle, and tan (the hounds). The pinstriped judges, sucking their pencils, look immensely stern and knowledgeable, which some manage better than others. All my friends tell me that I am a rotten bad judge but, by golly, I can look the part.

In the stands sit the cognoscenti, also sucking their pencils (psychologists please note the prevalence of the 'Deprived Sucking Syndrome' amongst hunting people). Every twist and turn of the judging is analyzed and criticized. You will hear much talk of 'shoulder slashes', 'second thighs', 'loins', and 'wheel backs'. You may deplore such language in mixed company – ah yes, there are many ladies present (for identification purposes, you may assume them to be the ones wearing floral hats) – but I assure you that these are merely technical terms relating to the physical characteristics of hounds.

Outside the ring the enthusiasts mingle. There is much back-slapping between friends, and narrowing of eyes between enemies. There is nothing like a little quiet character assassination on a warm summer's day. All the secrets of the hunting world are paraded, and, where truth fails, invention steps smartly into the breach. Did Luce-Rayne give up the mastership of the Blankshire because of ill health, or because he has had too many wives, and none of them his own? Is it true? have you heard? was old Lady Feele-Boote really doing that to the whipper-in? and not in the hound van, surely? A little gossip undoubtedly adds a little Worcestershire sauce to the Bloody Mary of life, and it gives one an appetite for luncheon.

I do not bother with luncheon in the course of my normal working life, but when I go out on the skite, it looms large. The luncheon at Harrogate used to be ghastly, and the service both tardy and innumerate. I have always claimed a major role in sharpening things up, and I am very pleased to say that our excellent caterer really had things up to snuff this year (salmon *en croute*, and seafood pasta). There was just the faintest whisper of problems with the Beaglers. The Beaglers have their show on a different day. Beaglers are different and it may be that they were promiscuously prodding the profiteroles. Whatever the cause, the caterer, a majestic retired cavalryman, rose mightily, and asked them if they still thought they were in the Sergeants' Mess: oh dear; it did cause a flutter.

The bitches are judged in the afternoon, and still there are old friends to greet, and to take lotion with. Old times are reminisced; old hunts rehunted; hounds, ancient and modern, are thoroughly discussed. Before you know it, it is time for the Championship, the presentation of the trophies and, if you can slip through the picket line of homeward-looking wives, just one more restoring glass.

A great summer outing – with hounds, friends and chatter; just do not believe any of the gossip you hear about *me*.

Chapter Seven

THE
MERRY-GO-ROUND
OF HAYMAKING

P ERHAPS YOU FANCY the idea of a bit of haymaking: the
swish of the scythe as your strong, sunburned arms drive
the blade through the rippling grasses; the lark singing high
above; the stone jar of cider waiting under the shady beech
tree; and, look, here comes Sweet Bessie, the milk maid. Stand
by for a bit of pastoral otium cum . . .

I have to tell you that the reality is different, more than
somewhat. For one thing, milk maids now have microchips on
their delicate shoulders: for seconds, haymaking is a time of
barely suppressed hysteria, frustration, and Giles's law, which
states that machinery is most likely to break down at the
moment when it is needed the most.

The trouble with making hay is the weather. The grass is
cut down, it then has to be killed; that is what hay is, grass
that has been killed, and cured. This process needs sunshine,
continuous hot sunshine, and a nice breeze to help things
along. The 'shear' should lie, untouched, gently cooking, for
five to six days, depending on the weather. It is then turned,
and turned again, until it is thoroughly sapless, dry, and fluffy,
with that sweet, unmistakable smell that tells of all the
goodness encapsulated within. At this stage it is put up into
swathes: the baler comes in and bales it; the loaders come in
and load it; and the elevators elevate it into the barn. Everyone
mops their brow and says, 'Cor Beggar, I could murder a pint.'
Cue grams, and fade into rustic sunset: piece of cake.

The trouble with making hay is the weather. Hands up
anyone who would like to guarantee seven consecutive dry

days in Britain, in the period mid June to mid August: I thought not.

First cut the hay: not a great problem, except for hitting the bit of old pram that someone has chucked into the mowing grass: return to farm, unbend the mower, and it starts to rain: miss two days.

Next turn the hay. On a nice day, with the doors off the tractor, and the pipe firing nicely, this is a pleasant job. The hay is spread, and spread again, so that sun and wind reaches every part. At this point it rains: return to farm, and watch cricket: rains stops play.

In an ordinary summer you can spend a couple of weeks getting your hay to the point of bailing, only to see it comprehensively resogged. It is not a good time to get asked for an increase in the housekeeping.

At last the baler appears in the field. It does two rounds, producing bales of every shape except the required cube: it chokes, vomits up a spew of cogs and shards of broken metal, and stops: it starts to rain. The fitter looks at the baler, sucks his teeth, and says that he has not seen one of those since he was a young apprentice. Spares? You've got to be joking, squire.

With every wetting and every turning, the hay loses goodness and feed value, so it is an anxious time. It is not much fun watching your winter feed slowly turning to slime beneath the relentless downpour.

Nearly everything flowers in the end. Hay of some sort will eventually reach the barn. One thing is certain: however bad the weather has been, the days when it is put in the barn will be unbearably hot and anyone who has worked on top of the stack, close below the corrugated iron roof of a dutch barn, will understand how agricultural thirsts are generated.

I have a much better system for hay these days: I ring up my Man of Hay, and order a lorry load when I want it. Then I spend the hay time watching the cricket – weather permitting, of course.

Chapter Eight

SPAIN
BY TRAIN

THE CHEAPEST WAY to travel from Northumberland to Spain is by charter flight from Newcastle upon Tyne. If it should so happen that you and your spouse are the only persons on the flight who do not belong to the Tyne and Wear 18-30 Club, then you may well decide to try the train next time. We went by train the next time.

There is no better way to start a railway journey than to travel on the Tyne Tees Pullman. This is the acceptable face of British Rail; clean, comfortable, courteous, and fast. There is time and space to enjoy an excellent breakfast, smoke a pipe, read the paper and get the day off to a good start. The traveller arrives in London refreshed, and with the day before him.

The Dover train is tired. It shows no enthusiasm for its work, and appears unloved and uncared for. It seems to have asthma, and arthritis. The train from Boulogne to Paris is kin to the Dover train, but it does at least provide drink.

I have no doubt that you will now be expecting the statutory eulogy about Paris. It was raining in Paris. Paris in the rain might as well be Bootle.

The Paris–Barcelona Talgo is an overnight job. I admired the substantial looking French rolling stock, and thought that the sleeping cars suggested a certain roomy comfort. As the Talgo expresses are the pride of Spanish Railways, I had high hopes for comfort there as well. The reality was a shock. The Talgo luxury carriages are the size and shape of the rolling stock on the Bakerloo Line. The first class sleeping compartments (two folding bunks) are the size of the average linen cupboard. They may represent luxury to small, neat Spaniards who can be packaged on minimal shelf space; for a 17-stone Englishman, they represent a challenge.

However, let us not despair; the dinner is excellent, the linen is clean, and the staff no more than surly. After dinner, the traveller is strongly advised to anaesthetize itself.

Dawn brings the foothills of the Pyrenees, and you can look forward to your breakfast. Do not allow the springing day to raise your hopes too high. The toast is leathery, the coffee is army surplus, and whatever the staff have been doing overnight has brought them no increase in happiness. You can only be pleased to arrive at Barcelona.

The original plan was to catch the midday Talgo to Valencia, which meant about a three hour wait at Barcelona. It was raining in Barcelona. There was a Transvia leaving for Valencia almost immediately; it seemed like a good idea at the time.

The Transvia is at the other end of the range from the Talgo. The average Transvia is on the verge of disintegration. The Spaniards love a good funeral so they pack the train in their hundreds so as to be in on the act. In honour of the occasion, the driver proceeds very slowly with his hand on the air horn. My theory is that this enables the emergency services to monitor his progress. Every so often despair seems to overcome the driver. He stops in the middle of nowhere and, with much shouting and gesticulating, leaves the train and has long animated conversations down trackside telephones; probably with his confessor. He then stands in the middle of the track, scratching himself rather intimately, presumably waiting for divine guidance. It is during these halts, with the temperature in the high seventies, and all the windows tightly shut, that one becomes aware of the authentic flavour of provincial Spain. We were very pleased to arrive at Valencia.

We went home by aeroplane.

Chapter Nine

SIGNS AND RITUALS

THE QUEUE WAS building up at the Spanish petrol pumps. The front car had been filled up, and the attendant was enjoying an animated and protracted conversation with the driver. The waiting began to fray the already sun-scorched nerves of the assembled Teutons, Saxons, Gauls and Latins who began to klaxon enthusiastically. From the offending car, an arm shot out and gave the assembled company *the finger*. As the car sped away, we were all interested to note that the driver, and passenger, were Holy Nuns.

This little incident made me think. The upward stabbing motion with the middle finger to denote abuse and derision is almost universal throughout the western world (including the US of A); the derivation of the gesture is priapically obvious, and requires no discussion. Why then do the British have to be different from their European brethren, and use two fingers when one would seem to do a workmanlike job?

I am now in a position to satisfy your intense curiosity. Most of you will remember Crécy, Agincourt, and the period when the English bowmen laid waste the flower of French chivalry. This caused not a little ill feeling amongst the French which was aggravated by the fact that the behaviour of the English, off the field of play, left a lot to be desired. The first two fingers of the right hand are the ones normally used to draw a bow with, and it became the French custom to remove these important fingers from any English bowmen they happened to lay their hands on. There was always a bit of pre-match hype before the battles of those days, and it became the custom for the English bowmen to demonstrate to the opposing team that both vital fingers were attached, and in full working order.

There is a form of rural greeting that used to puzzle me a bit. It consists of twisting your head to one side, and winking as you pass someone on the road. It occurs to me that if you are driving a horse and cart, and have your hands full of reins, then this is a very sensible way of greeting a passing acquaintance. The horse and cart have gone the way of the long bow, but the form remains.

There are little verbal rituals, too. When the last bale comes off the trailer, or the last sheep goes through the pens, someone will always say, 'That's the one we should have started with.'

In the days of pounds, shillings and pence, I used to frequent a certain Wessex public house. There were two very old men who were regular customers. Every evening when they got their first pint, they would perform the same ritual:

'I looks to you.'

'I has your eye.'

'I bows to you': he bows.

'I likewise bows, winks, and drinks according.'

The whole thing was executed with great solemnity, and was quite a feature of the place. The old men swore that it was a Wessex toast of great antiquity; it certainly got them a lot of free pints, which might also be a tradition of great antiquity.

Chapter Ten

RIDING THE
HILLS

I WANT YOU to know about my ATV (All Terrain Vehicle). When I bought it, I felt that it was one of the most interesting things to have happened to me in recent years; rather like the Male Menopause. It may be that there are some of you, out there, who are unfamiliar with ATVs; I do not suppose that you find many of them illegally parked in Knightsbridge, or slumbering quietly beside the BMW in a Macclesfield driveway. The ATV is a four-wheeled motor bicycle with large low ground pressure tyres. My pride and joy has a 350-cc engine, high and low ratio gears, and permanent four-wheel drive: it is a formidable beast.

Sometimes my duties take me up into the hills, and require me to cover considerable distances (like twenty, or thirty miles) over country that rises to 2500 feet, and is inaccessible to conventional motor vehicles. To walk is immensely good for the figure, and the wind, but is also very slow; and you do not want to be carrying very much.

I have used horses, and still do, on occasion. The problem with the horse is that much of the ground is more suitable for navigation than equitation. Also, if you do get to where you want to be, and want to stop and do something whilst you are there, you either have to have someone else to hold the horse, or you have to have a horse that is not going to lose interest, and wander off; like all the way home.

Enter the ATV (who is known as Rupert, for a reason that I will explain later). Rupert has a box on the back which will carry my bait bag, oilskins, feed sacks, spades, fencing tools, and a dog; but not necessarily in that order. There is also a cunningly contrived length of plastic tubing into which my stick is inserted. A Citizens' Band Wireless is clegged on the front to maintain contact with base. In case any of you Breakers out there are interested, my Handle is 'Frantic Ferret'.

The first bit, up an access road, is fairly smooth and straightforward, and the dog is happy to sit on the bag and look over my shoulder. At the last gate she jumps off because she knows that, from hereon out, the going gets rough. The higher up we go, the rougher and wetter the going is. The machine has ten forward gears to play with, and I suspect that it would grind up almost any gradient short of the vertical. It is only limited by my nerve, which is a rather delicate plant; like its owner.

The hill is streaked with 'sheep drains' which were hand dug, in the past, to remove surplus moisture. Skilled shepherding motor-bicyclists simply open up the throttle, and jump them. The ATV requires a different technique. The drain is approached slowly, and the front wheels dropped gently into the drain; a burst on the throttle pulls the front wheels out, and lets the back wheels drop in; another quick burst, and we are out, out and away.

On the hill tops, the peat hags lie in wait: a giant sponge that soaks up the rain, and then squeezes it out into the streams below. During particularly wet weather, this ground is impassable for horses, and difficult even for two-wheeled motor bicycles. Rupert's great low pressure tyres make nothing of all but the very wettest ground; so far, I have only managed to get stugged once, and then we reversed out fairly easily.

Bull snouts are the worst. These expanses of closely grouped grass tussocks are a misery to ride over. Every turn of the wheel is felt through every inch of the body: it is very good for the figure.

One morning I had ground my way high up in the hills. The going had varied from 'rough a bit' (worse) to 'bad a bit' (much worse), but we made it. I lay in the heather, the bitch and I had just had our bacon butty, the thermos was to hand, and the pipe was drawing nicely. Far below the local foxhounds were busy in a big bracken bed. Before me was mile upon mile of rolling hill, frantic with racing cloud shadows. The breeze was fresh, the sun was warm, and I was mightily content. There are no short cuts to happiness, but sometimes you get there quicker on an ATV.

Chapter Eleven

BORDER CROSSINGS

THERE ARE A LOT of Hopes in this part of the world. How then, you may ask, does that make us different from Carshalton, or Kingsbury Episcopi, where people also may well have dreams, and aspirations? In this context, Hope is a derivation of the Old English word Hop, meaning a valley. Life in the valleys has not always been full of wine and roses, as you can tell from names like Bleakhope (pronounced Blake-up), and Sourhope (pronounced Surrup).

The inhabitants of these valleys may well have found life difficult. Not only would both places have been hard living, but they were both handy for one of the old main roads between England and Scotland: the Salters' Way. This road is now a quiet, grassy track, but in the bad old days of the Border Wars, it was one of the hot spots; part of it is still known as the Thieves Road. Thus, if the lads of Ryle, Prendwick, and Scrainwood were away across the border to replenish the store cupboard, they would be sure to call on Sourhope on the way for a bit of the raping and pillaging, which the custom of the time called for, however boring they may have found it. By the same token, when the Bold Boys of Bowmont came over the hill for the return match, they would hardly neglect to bring a little more misery into the lives of the inhabitants of Bleakhope.

Before the amalgamation of the Scottish and English thrones, this part of the world can never have been dull: cross-border pillage and rustling were the major local industries: treachery, feud and murder were rife. Today the whole thing has been sublimated into Rugby Football: I do not know what there is in the rule book about Rape and Pillage, but I am pretty certain that Murder is discouraged. I have no doubt that someone will let me know if this is not the case.

The names of the great 'riding' clans are still prominent in this area. To the best of my knowledge, the famous Spur of the Charltons still hangs at Hesleyside. When the larder was getting a bit bare, it was the custom for the Charlton matriarch of the moment to bring the spur in on a dish as the family all sat at table, with knife and fork at the high port. The men would then sigh deeply, tighten their belts, saddle their horses, and set off across the border for a bit of bulk acquisition.

The Robsons of Redesdale also went shopping and, one dark night, lifted a whole flap of sheep off the Grahams. They were very cross to find, in the cold light of day, that the sheep had the 'scab'. It is obviously the height of bad manners, and poor form, for your neighbours to allow you to steal scabby sheep off them. The Robsons were rightly put out. To emphasize the breach of etiquette, they returned across the border and hanged nine Grahams: a sort of early Consumer Protection scheme.

Other local place names record these stirring days. I do not know exactly what happened at Murdercleugh, but it was obviously not a game of bridge – although now I come to think of it . . .

I do know what happened at Skirl Naked. Some of the Scots at Flodden suddenly remembered that they had to get home early, having very likely left the gas on. They took a wrong turning in Wooler, and got wet crossing the Harthope Burn. So they stripped off, and danced a reel to get dry. It did them no good. The English caught up with them at Bloody-bush Edge, which got its name that day. I have always maintained that Scottish dancing is injurious to health.

Chapter Twelve

THE
KELSO SHEEP
SALE

IN EARLY AUTUMN, sheepmen from all parts of Her Majesty's realm head for Kelso. This attractive little border town lies athwart the River Tweed. It is an important commercial centre and is also outwith (we are in Scotland) Floors Castle, the pile of the dashing Duke of Roxburghe. Kelso is also host to the biggest annual sale of rams in Britain; and if you want lambs, then you have got to have rams (called tups in this part of the world).

Not a bad life being a tup: you get fed and cosseted, and then every year you get six weeks of intensive nooky. I wonder how many of us mere humans can claim as much: not I, sir, for one. There is a snag to this idyll: after about four years, a tup is reckoned to have shot his bolt (if you will pardon the choice of words), and goes off to become Mutton Vindaloo, whilst the farmer goes seeking a younger replacement.

Some ten thousand people converge on Kelso every year. They come from Cornwall and Caithness; from Nantgwynant and Norwich. They do not all come to buy and sell: for many it is a great day out amongst other people for whom sheep are also a way of life.

I came to a reluctant policy decision this year, to get rid of Bert and Barney, my two Oxford Down tups. They are good tups and produce strong, big-framed lambs but, sadly, these are just not the sort of lambs that the butchers want these days. Whilst I enjoy keeping sheep, I also have to be commercial and do my best to ensure that the sheep do their bit by helping to keep me. So I set out for Kelso with my horn heid stick, my sandwiches and my cheque book.

The two most popular sires in the sheep world at the moment (for sheepmen are very fashion conscious), are the Suffolk which looks like a suet pudding on short legs, and the Blue-Faced Leicester which is all legs, head and neck: it has been well described as a sheep that appears to have been designed by a committee. The Suffolk is a terminal sire, which means that it produces a lamb for the butcher. The BFL set onto a hill ewe, produces the prolific Mule ewe, the mainstay of the national breeding flock.

What I wanted this time was something that might just produce me ewe lambs to sell on, and a wether lamb for the butcher. I walked straight past the massed ranks of Suffolks. No, that is not correct, nor would it have been possible, because people whom I know and like kept hailing me and importuning me to look at their sheep. Politeness and prudence compelled me to show an interest; otherwise they might have pelted me with the cabbages which they use to stuff their great soggy brutes. You may feel that I am somewhat pre-judiced about the Suffolk breed; this is true. I used to have Suffolk tups and their progeny appeared to come into the world with a stubborn determination to leave it again as soon as possible.

At the back of the ground, behind the gents, is ring 15 where the continental breeds and crosses are furtively sold: it was to here that I made my stately progress – but not without being comprehensively nipped on the way. A nip is a small measure of whisky, without which no form of social intercourse on the borders is deemed valid.

The selling at Kelso is a miracle of organisation. There are no less than sixteen rings and thirteen firms of auctioneers, all selling simultaneously. The same firm may have lots selling in four different rings at the same time. Some pretty nifty leg work on the part of the individual auctioneers is required: a portly running auctioneer is a gladsome sight. But, before you get too sorry for them, just work out their commission on 1.75 million smackers which was the turnover this year: let them sweat a bit for it.

I was seeking a Bleu du Maine cross. A Bleu du Maine is a French breed, as you may have guessed. They produce big-framed, vigorous lambs with lots of good lean meat in all the right places. I had bought two pure breds at the breed sale the year before — at a price that made my teeth crunch: something a little cheaper was in order. I managed to buy two decent lambs for £260 and £280. To put this figure in perspective, you need to know that the top price at the sale was £4,600. I wonder, sir, if your loved one values you so highly.

Chapter Thirteen

A HUNTSMAN'S
REPUTATION

IF YOU HAVE THE better sort of diary it will tell you that the foxhunting season starts on 1 November. The diary is correct, but most packs will have been hunting for some time before. Autumn hunting starts as soon as the harvest is finished. The hounds up here will have been on the job since 10 August.

Autumn hunting is a daybreak operation with a few people to help but not enough to hinder. This gives the hunt staff time and space to get the annual entry of young hounds settled into their work before the start of the season proper.

With the beginning of the season comes the OPENING MEET – which is in capital letters because it is a great occasion. It is the formal opening of the new season, and everyone gets a bit over-excited about it. The opening meet is a time for full fig; the newest red, or black, coats; breeches of a snowy whiteness; boots boned and buffed to a mirror-like brilliance, and if your spurs are upside down, it will cost you a round of drinks. The hunting cap is generally worn these days, but the traditional, well-groomed silk hat still has its place on some traditional, well-groomed heads.

Horses will not only be highly polished, but will be full of corn and early season vim; the riders will be far from fit, but will be full of early season nerves which may require a little emollient specific: the combination can lead to complications, and to rather untidy partnership dissolutions. A well-shaken peer once complained to his stud groom that his horses were getting too much corn, to which the old retainer replied that whoever was getting too many oats it certainly was not the horses.

The biggest dose of nerves will be reserved for the hunt staff; their nerve ends will be as highly polished as their equipment. Part of the fascination of hunting a pack of hounds is that it is an immensely difficult thing to do well. There is an old saying amongst huntsmen that 'a huntsman's reputation is only as good as his last day's hunting'; his reputation, and his neck, are on the line every hunting day and both are more easily injured than repaired.

The opening meet is especially gut-shrivelling for the huntsman, for several reasons. One is the number of people on horse, foot and car who will turn out for the big occasion, all desperate for good sport. A second reason is that opening meets tend to be held in places hallowed by tradition, but not necessarily any longer much use for hunting: motorways on two sides, and an Urban Resettlement Area on a third can cramp the style a bit. The third reason is that hunting is dependant on the hounds being able to smell the fox's scent, as we rather quaintly call it. Scent depends largely on the weather conditions, and the state of the barometer. In general terms a steady, or rising glass, is good for hunting; a falling glass is bad (especially if there is any whisky left in it). November tends to be an unsettled month.

Many thousands of people attend opening meets throughout Great Britain each November. If you were to ask them why they were there, they might offer a variety of explanations, but the main reasons would be that hunting is part of their way of life, and they enjoy it.

Chapter Fourteen

THE
ALWINTON BORDER
SHEPHERDS' SHOW

THROUGHOUT THE COUNTRY, there are places that have come to be regarded as social and cultural centres for the areas that surround them: Bath springs to mind, as do York and Harrogate; and then there is Alwinton. The fact that most of you have never heard of the place is entirely your loss.

Alwinton lies at the confluence of the rivers of Coquet and Alwin. It is also the point where three of the main England/ Scotland roads converge; it matters not that no one uses these roads now except walkers and shepherds (I do not recommend you to attempt them in the family Porsche), they are there. Alwinton is the nerve centre of a huge area of wild rolling hills, with lonely steadings scattered about them. It is made up of a farm, some 'twenty houses, and the Rose and Thistle. To call the Rose and Thistle a pub is much too simple rather like calling a desert oasis, a pond: it is a centre for all that is best in border culture – music, story telling, crack (conversation) and, just occasionally, a glass of something restorative and medicinal: it is a busy place.

The flow of culture is continuous, but there are probably three events that turn the flow into a torrent. These are: Alwinton Show, the New Year's Day meet of the hounds, and the Shepherds' Supper in March.

The Alwinton Border Shepherds' Show happens in the autumn. On the face of it, it is just a local show with all the usual items: sheep, dressed sticks, produce; there will be a leavening of entertaining items like wrestling, a hill race (foot), and a hound trail; there is also a small fun fair and trade stands.

Every year some 4000 people flock to the rushy field below the village. It has become a traditional day out for the pitmen of the north-east and their families; coach loads come from Ashington, Bedlington and Durham. At the same time, sheep men come pouring out of the lonely border valleys.

When so many moving parts are gathered together in one fairly small space, lubrication is necessary. The Rose and Thistle is a pint pot bearing a quart of humanity throughout the day; by evening the atmosphere could be cut into blocks. In addition there is a Barnum-and-Baily sized marquee on the show ground devoted entirely to dispensing spiritual refreshment; there is no waiter service, and experience as a prop forward is helpful in winning through to the bar. It is in the marquee that young men demonstrate their upward mobility by climbing one of the poles and seeing how far they can get out on the horizontal ridge pole. Your correspondent used to be rather a dab hand at this, until the awful day when his braces became inextricably entangled with the ring thing at the top of the pole, which meant that he was not the only thing to come down (to cries of 'Hello Cheeky').

In some years, I am in demand as a judge, of the trail hounds no less. If you are unfamiliar with hound trailing it is thus: an aniseed trail is laid in advance over some ten miles of hill; the hounds are then loosed off to run the trail, and the first one home is the winner: simple.

Trail hounds were originally based on foxhounds, but have now been bred, or in-bred, into a fairly distinct type. The stamina points have been sacrificed for pace. They are clipped, burnished and fed on secret recipes. They carry absolutely no spare flesh and an immense amount of spare cash. Betting is what it is all about and hundreds, or even thousands, of pounds in bets are involved. The judge who calls the winner incorrectly will find both his decision and his parentage being questioned *con brio*. It is a job that calls for quick decisions and strong nerves.

The hounds are set away and disappear into the hills. The spectators disperse and wander off to see some other part of the show. If he has got any sense, the judge goes in search of some whisky.

(Whilst we are waiting, perhaps I should tell you of a sad occasion at a hound trail in Cumberland. A young couple had settled in the lee of a stone wall; I understand that it was their intention to study the poetry of the great Mr Wordsworth. It was perhaps unfortunate that the spot they chose happened to be on the hound trail from the local show. This meant that they were interrupted in mid stanza by thirty trail hounds landing on them from the wall top.)

Half an hour later, the spectators start to gather at the finish line. Owners and handlers are penned back behind a rope. They are equipped with whistles, flags, tin cans, rattles and klaxons. The judge strides to the finish post in an important and spiritful manner. He is surrounded by six very large men: these are the official catchers. There are no number cloths on trail hounds. As they cross the finish line, the judge will shout: 'The Brindle! Black Spot! The Roan! . . .' The catcher will then sprint across to his designated hound and mark it until the details can be garnered from the proud owner. The catchers can also be useful as a security detail for the judge were he to muddle his roans.

Now all eyes are on a distant hillside. Massed binoculars scan. 'They're coming!' and a long line of distant light-coloured dots can be seen. They are moving fast. I suppose trail hounds must average about 20 mph over rough country. The Noise begins. Each owner has his own method of spurring his hound to great efforts: screams, whistles, rattles, flags, klaxons. The judge crouches by his post and bellows out the order as the hounds cross the finish line. The catchers rush forward and the hounds receive tit bits out of billy-cans for their efforts.

There are usually six races in all, and then it is back to the judges' caravan for some grave discussion of the Lamb Variable Premium. A man I bought a stick off insisted that we should cement the bargain in the Rose and Thistle. The evening of the Alwinton Show became a feast of reason and a flow of soul; I think. There was music and singing, I should not wonder. Yes, I am certain of it. That is my decision, and it is final – for was I not as sober as a judge?

Chapter Fifteen

CLOTHES FOR
FIELD CREDIBILITY

I HAVE BEFORE ME a glossy magazine advertisement showing a nice young couple (mixed, you may be relieved to hear) all dressed up in what admen conceive to be suitable clothes for Rural Life. I just wonder whether they have got it right. Take the gel for starters. Her dashing and colourful get up might be all very well for spring in Swiss Cottage; for ferreting in the teeth of a black north-easter it would be complete frost, and I use the word advisedly.

I do not see her charming companion faring much better. The boreal blast is going to ruin his blow wave, and he will be sorry he ever got out of the car in those shoes. What is needed in these advertisements is a little more reality. If people really want to know about Backwoods Chic, they can do no better than to consult me, one of the sharpest dressers in the boondocks. You would no doubt like to have a little preview of what will be *in*.

Hats are important. You should have several and change them according to weather and mood. My normal hat is a tweed cap rather like a large muffin but not as shapely. All caps should have a bit of grease about them.

The face is vitally important, and the chaps in the magazines really fall down on this one. The face should be jolly shades of red and purple with lots of dinky little broken veins. This interesting colour scheme should cease abruptly half way up the forehead where the cap comes; above this, the skin should be fish-belly white. I have to tell you that it takes thirty years of wind, weather and whisky to get a genuine Arcadian countenance. I have no doubt that the cosmetic people will rise to the challenge (Feral Foundation Cream, perhaps).

Any pullover will do, *but* it must have no elbows and smell of sheep. The personality can be allowed to flower a little when it comes to the jacket. The waxed cotton jacket has been much in favour. I do not like them because whilst they keep the wet out, they also keep it in. My dears, you must let the body *breathe*. Stick to wool/cotton; that is my advice.

For genuine Field Credibility the contents of the pockets are almost more important than the jacket itself. I will empty my pockets on the desk for your inspection. We have a lambsfoot knife, a thing for cleaning pipes, a pipe, a tobacco pouch, three crushed boxes of matches, three throat lozenges (engrimed), nuts and bolts (assorted), a bill for sheep feed with something written on the back which I cannot read, a hypodermic syringe, a bottle of long-acting penicillin, half a chocolate biscuit (partworn) and string, fluff, and something black and sticky that might once have been Stockholm Tar; but then again, it might not.

Trousers should be generous both in conception and execution. By which I mean that there should be plenty of room for air to circulate, and the wearer should be able to bend or sit without fear of emasculation. At least one knee should be patched. Twenty-four-inch bottoms are obligatory.

Backwoodsmen are very keen on their feet, and give much thought to boots. I wear shepherding boots. These boots, made by a few specialists in the north, are the definitive walking boot: they 'lace through to the toe' and the ends curl up for going up hill; they bristle with hob nails. Mine weigh out at three and a half pounds a piece. Once you get them started, they walk themselves and, with a little practice, you can usually get them stopped within a hundred yards.

If my ideas catch on, there is going to be much fluttering in the dovecote of rural fashion. I am very much afraid that most of those male models will have to go. It would be a pity, however, to waste the talents of all those pretty ladies. I suppose that I shall just have to educate them in the ways of the Backwoods.

Chapter Sixteen

THE ATTRACTION OF HUNTING

WHO GOES HUNTING? If your knowledge of hunting was entirely gleaned from the tabloid press, you would think that the hunting field was entirely staffed by Old Etonian cavalry officers. There is a grain of truth here in as much as it is probable that majority of OECOs hunt, but they make up only a tiny percentage of the half-million people who hunt regularly in Britain. People who follow hounds come from all socio-economic groupings (they used to be called classes), and from town as well as from the country. I heard of a hunt whose following included a doctor, a vet, a nurse, a dentist, and a priest: all eventualities catered for.

It is probably true to say that you will not find many Labour Party activists in the hunting field. Some hunting people still vote Labour, but a larger number switched their political allegiance after the League Against Cruel Sports bought a slice of the Labour Party Manifesto.

There has been a tremendous upsurge in support for hunting during the last thirty years. When I started hunting seriously in the 1950s, hunting was geriatric and appeared to be sliding into a terminal coma. Times have changed and there are many more young people hunting. In my own hunt, the average age would somewhere in the thirties. There are also many 'new' people hunting, people who do not come from traditional sporting backgrounds. This has created problems. Hunting takes place only by the good will of the farmers and land owners; their interests must be paramount. This means that the physical numbers of 'hooves on the ground' that any given area can cope with are finite. Many hunts in the more populous areas of the country have reached saturation point, and have waiting lists for mounted followers.

Not everyone hunts on a horse, although it is interesting to note that the equine population is thought to be higher in the last few years than it was in 1914. You do not have to be rich to hunt, but you do need to be reasonably well off to keep a horse in hunting trim: you will see little change out of £2000 per annum.

For every mounted person, there are something like 250 unmounted followers. They hunt by car, bicycle and on foot, and are often the most dedicated hunting people. The cross-country ride is of no interest to them, although a good view of a comprehensive fall does add spice to their day. For the non-riders seeing the fox, and watching the hounds work, is what it is all about. Many of them are immensely knowledge-able in the art of venery, and even if they are not, lack of knowledge certainly does nothing to inhibit strongly expressed opinions.

The urge to hunt is as old as man, and is quite as basic as certain other urges which do not come within the scope of this column. I am always slightly puzzled when people ask me why I hunt; they might as well ask me why I eat and drink. If pressed further, I might say that hunting is exciting, and that the fox and the foxhound are two of the nicest people I know; which just might tend to confuse the questioner further. Therefore allow me to offer another man's reason for hunting:

'The attraction of hunting is that it acts on the mind like a poultice on a sore.' I hope that that will do for you to be going on with. Who said it? A chap called Leon Trotsky; obviously a very sound man, whoever he was.

Chapter Seventeen

OVER THE JUMPS

IF YOU HUNT ON A horse, you are at some point going to be faced with the prospect of jumping something. It is a prospect that has always appalled me (me being one of nature's wimps), but many people salivate at the prospect of a line of big, black fences.

The sort of obstacle you meet will very much depend on which part of Britain you hang your hat in. Let us start in the Celtic mists of the far west. Fences usually depend on climate and the materials to hand. In Cornwall and Ireland there is lots of stone and lots of earth, and there used to be lots of time. From these three useful commodities came banks. The principle of bank jumping is that the horse jumps onto the top of the bank, does something clever with its feet and jumps off the other side. Some banks are wide enough for you and the horse to pause on the top and look at the view. In Ireland the view sometimes contains a man wearing a double-breasted gun, in which case you have time to turn round and return whence you came. Most banks now have a strand of barbed wire on each side, and a mini jungle on the top, which must add spice to the leap; if you like spice.

In the south and middle of England the heavy soil is conducive to the growth of thorn which makes a good fence. Thorn fences are now usually cut mechanically. In the old days they used to be 'cut and laid': the stems cut partly through and then laid horizontally so that they continued to grow. The fence was strengthened with vertical stakes and a plaited binder on the top. In wetter parts, there would be a ditch on one or both sides, and to stop the cattle getting in the ditch, there would be an ox rail made of good solid split oak. Your thrusting rider would therefore have been confronted with a rail, a ditch, a solid cut and lay, a ditch, and another solid rail: this was called a double oxer. The experts maintained that it was not possible to jump more than twelve consecutively without having a fall. Now the ox rail has been replaced with barbed wire, and the ditch dug out with a mechanical digger, making the whole thing quite unjumpable; for which relief much thanks. Thorn fences that you can jump require a certain amount of impetus because of the ditches.

Lying in a ditch with a horse on top of you is a dismal way of passing the time: I know. It is even more dismal in a rhyne. In certain low-lying parts of the country the fields are divided by waterfilled dykes, or rhynes. The water is stagnant and covers unmeasured feet of ooze. If your horse gets in one, you will need a tractor and ropes to get it out. If you happen to be underneath the horse then you may just have a problem.

Drystone walls are a feature of many of our uplands. Horses usually jump stone walls well for the same reason that they jump solid post and rails well: the obstacles command respect.

Most horses can be trained to jump wire — always provided that the rider's nerve is equal to the task. I once bought a cob called Snotty. The first time I hunted him was after taking on too much port wine at the meet. I presented him at five strands of barbed wire, and he never rose an inch. If you hit barbed wire hard and fast enough, it may snap. You and your horse may also turn base over apex. Snotty jumped wire beautifully thereafter, but I am not sure that my training method was the correct one.

Over the years I have had many falls. I have been rolled on, lain on, stepped on, and jumped on (by horses). There is no jumping on our lovely open Cheviot hills, and that suits me down to the ground; if you see what I mean.

Chapter Eighteen

TRADITIONAL
NORTHERN ENTERTAINMENT

So WHAT DO I DO in the long northern winter nights? Left
to my own inclinations I bank up the fire and settle down
with a book, a pipe, and something nourishing in a glass. This
is regarded locally as subversive behaviour; going out is the
thing to do. If the local quality feel like a bit of rough trade, I
sometimes get asked out to drink their port, but as I tend to
drink an awful lot of it, and dribble as well, the invitations are
rather widely spaced.

The other main interruptions to my otium cum often seem
to involve singing and dancing. There is a tremendous tradition
of music in this part of the world. After it has been packaged
and sanitized, it will appear in the south as 'folk' music, and
will be performed in polytechnic nasal by ladies with hairy
armpits and dungarees. By then, it is 'culsher'; up here it is still
just the local music, and is very much a living thing.

Just down the road from me lives one of the greatest
traditional fiddlers. He spent all his working life as a hill
shepherd on remote steadings. He is a musician and composer
in the very highest class – but has only three fingers on his
left hand: think about it. Down the road the other way lives
the best concertina player I have ever heard; he also plays the
Northumbrian pipes and the penny whistle, and travels all
over the world. It may be that you are unfamiliar with the
Northumbrian pipes. The bag is inflated by a bellows arrangement worked by the right elbow. They produce a lovely,
gentle, mellow, but exciting noise suitable for the great
indoors. Many of the prominent local musicians are getting on

a bit in years, but there are plenty of good young people carrying on the tradition of playing and composing. One of the best fiddlers I heard lately was a pulchritudinous girl of twenty years. The inspiration for the music and the songs still comes from the life and work in the wild border hills.

It is a lasting regret to me that I cannot play any instrument except a mouth organ (very badly). However, I am blessed with a quite creditable bar-room baritone – at least, I am told it is a baritone; I would not know one if I saw it in the window of the Glanton shop. Once I have been given enough whisky I can be persuaded to sing. It might be more correct to say that it is very difficult to prevent me from singing when in my cups; I suppose that it is better than getting quarrelsome and/or amorous. I also have a certain novelty value as the Only Singing Master of Foxhounds in Northumberland, so one way and another I get 'called out' quite often at Shepherds' Suppers, and other occasions where musical entertainment is on the menu.

The other evening I sat in a smoke-filled room with some two hundred other men; we had all supped and sipped well. We were listening to one of the great local performers, and there was not so much as a scrape of a chair or the chink of a glass, so gripped were the audience. The applause at the end was thunderous. I cannot claim to attract such concentration or applause, but it is a very great privilege to be asked to perform alongside the people who can.

New Year's Eve does not happen in the borders; it is regarded as an effete southern custom like wearing thermal vests, or going shopping with the wife. Up here there is Old Year's Night, and it is different.

I live at one end of a valley. Whatever the valley may be called on the map, its local name is Whisky Valley. Whisky Valley is populated by charming and hospitable people, and on Old Year's Night these desirable qualities come to flash point. Many farms keep open house over the new year, and some peripatetic revellers may not see their own hearth, home or bed for two or three days. In spite of all this activity, the stock still get fed and the sheep looked at – although counting may present a problem at times. There is nothing like fresh air, exercise and a major cowp (fall) off the motorbike to get the system back into good working order for another bout of hospitality. Old Year's Night is a test of stamina and survival; having fun is a serious business. Somewhere along the line there is likely to be singing, music, and (heaven preserve me) dancing.

Singing is much more my hand cart: it can be done sitting down with a glass in the hand, and therefore much to be preferred to dancing. As I have said, there are many gifted singers and musicians in these parts, and it is a guinea to a gooseberry that you are going to fall in with a number of them somewhere during Old Year's Night. Occasionally I get asked to do my party piece; usually a song called *The Threshing Machine* which comes from Dorset. It is a song about lust and other agricultural matters, and so is probably very appropriate for the occasion.

The trouble with Old Year's Night is that it becomes New Year's Day. With or without benefit of bed, it soon comes time to feed the ewes, and to pull on the breeches and boots for the New Year's meet of the hounds at the Rose and Thistle. This is a Great Occasion, and may not be missed. There are any number of hands to be shaken before the hounds can move off, and it is not possible to shake a hand without having a drink with its owner: offence must not be given. However, a good day's hunting does wonders for the liver. It is just unfortunate if, like last year, it comes on to snow heavily, and at two o'clock one is faced with the prospect of either going home or returning to the Rose and Thistle and getting snowed in: a truly difficult decision.

Chapter Nineteen

THE HEARTLAND OF
RURAL FRANCE

IF YOU TRAVEL to Clermont-Ferrand, there is one thing that
you should not do, and two things that you should. The
negative first: do not fly from Paris by Air Inter unless you
relish acute discomfort. I will tell you that the plane concerned
is an elderly Fokker and leave it at that.

In Clermont-Ferrand you *must* stay at the Hotel Radio,
which is in fact in the suburb of Royat. For starters, it is very
quiet, not being stuck on the main drag; in addition, it is
everything that an hotel ought to be and so seldom is. It is
spotlessly clean, simple and comfortable.

Like all the best hotels it is a family concern. Madame
Mioche handles the administration and I opine that she runs a
pretty tight ship: everything, including the staff, sparkles. The
browsing and sluicing is of a very high order, and you can do
no better than to put yourself entirely in the hands of M.
Mioche who, like a true artist, will conjure up a memorable
culinary entertainment for you. The Radio is the only hotel I
have found in recent years to which I would look forward to returning.

The next thing you should do in Clermont-Ferrand is to
leave it as quickly as possible for the Bourbonnais. If your
immediate reaction is to reach for a map, look for Vichy and
Moulins. You will see that you are about as near the centre of
France as can be, and the Bourbonnais could well be described
as the heartland of rural France.

It may be that your ideal French holiday comprises a
frenetic night life, basting bodies, and ladies who would have

been much better advised to have kept their tops on; in this case, the Bourbonnais is not for you. However, if you seek tranquillity and a taste of proper French country life then you are on the right track.

It is a secret land, more pleasant than startling, a land of great woodlands of oak and birch. The French have been much better at preserving their ancient woodlands than the British. A French forest teems with animal and birdlife, and there is the pleasure of walking on a leaf bed as old as the forest. On the sandy tracks, you will find feetings of red and roe deer; an experienced forester can tell the age, size and sex of the animal from the slots. This area is also a stronghold of the wild boar. The Rallye Chapeau hunt this area: they are one of the most famous packs of Boarhounds in France. French hunting still preserves the ancient traditions of Venery. There you can see, and hear, the French horn being put to its original, practical use.

Between the woodlands are rolling grazing lands with white Charollais cattle and Isle de France and Charollais sheep. British flockmasters keep in fashion by using Charollais and Bleu du Maine rams; the French crave our Suffolks. The countryside reminded me of parts of Dorset; rolling grassland with secret streams in the bottoms. There are miles of winding, deserted (different in this respect from modern Dorset) lanes with isolated farmsteads and tiny villages where dogs can still sleep in the middle of the road.

The Bourbonnais is an area of large estates with many lovely houses and châteaux, some of which are open to the public. I have vivid memories of a hunt dinner at the Château du Vieux Chambord, near Jaligny. This old and beautiful house is still very much a home. It is the home of M. Devaulx de Chambord, whose family have been there since 1276. The guide book says *'visites tolerées'*. It is a fascinating place.

The de Tracy family have been at Paray-le-Fresil for some five hundred years. Mme la Marquise is a driving force in promoting tourism for the area and in setting up 'La France des Villages' which has details of a large number of farmhouses and self-catering apartments in the area. I can thoroughly recommend Paray-le-Fresil.

Most people ignore the centre of France in their lemming-like rush to the polluted Mediterranean. If your idea of a holiday is good food, friendly people, and peace and quiet, then the Bourbonnais could well be for you. Although now that I have discovered it I do not want too many of you going down there and spoiling it.

One last word: the local pear brandy is very good, but approach it with caution.

Chapter Twenty

THE PAGEANTRY OF BOAR HUNTING

I HAD NEVER SEEN a wild boar before I was introduced to Kiki. Kiki, together with Madame Kiki and their numerous offspring, lives in a large enclosure in an oak forest in the Bourbonnais. He is about the size of a shetland pony and likes having his tummy scratched. However, I would never disregard the tusks of considerable length and great sharpness. Kiki and the forest are owned by Madame la Comtesse de Monspey (hereinafter referred to as Madame). Madame keeps him and his family because she loves the wild pigs and likes to watch and study them. Madame is also the owner and master of the Rallye Chapeau, one of the best-known packs of boarhounds in France. Like all true hunters, she has great affection and respect for the quarry she hunts. To be nearer the heart of things, Madame recently shut up her château and moved herself and her hounds to a lovely but rather run down farm in the middle of the forest. With a proper sense of priority she did up the kennels before starting on the house, and camped in the bothy while the renovations took place.

There are some three hundred packs of hounds in France, and the number is increasing. There are 35 packs of staghounds, 73 packs of foxhounds, 61 packs hunting roe deer, 114 packs of hare hounds, and 14 packs of boarhounds. There is some resistance to hunting amongst elements of the political left, but there is overwhelming and very enthusiastic support amongst the rural population. In Britain, country people are becoming a persecuted minority but in France the rural vote is important, and politicians still have to heed the wishes of the countryman.

The Rallye Chapeau hangs its hat (my first bilingual pun) about as near the centre of France as you can get. The Bourbonnais is an area largely ignored by English visitors; it is unspoilt and friendly, and the food is superb. I found my way there thanks to the good offices of Sir Rupert Buchanan-Jardine, Bt, MFH, who is the only Briton who knows about, and is respected in, the French hunting world. Old soldiers know how to find good billets, and we received great kindness and hospitality from the Marquis and Marquise de Tracy.

Your average wild boar is a meandering animal and feeds over a wide area. He may spend a day in one wood and be lying up fifteen miles away the next morning. For this reason, it is no good just trolling off to any old wood and trusting to luck to find a boar; you have to *faire le bois*. 'Doing the wood', or harbouring as we would call it, happens thus. Some twenty people meet early in the morning at a pre-arranged spot. Each person is issued with an old and wise hound on a leash, to provide confirmation of the suspected presence of pig. Each team is detailed off to a particular area.

At 0700 I presented myself at the kennels for just the merest smackerel: two goose eggs, a plate of ham, bread, cheese, pâté (boar), coffee, wine and eau de vie; sets a chap up for the day.

At 0730 I departed with Toby, the son of the house. Toby, in his turn, handed me into the genial custody of Monsieur le Général Lorrain and a hound called Rocambole. For two hours, we tramped the rides in these beautiful woods looking for feetings and other signs. We did find places where pig had been rootling, but they were not fresh. There were no fresh signs. We went back to the rendezvous slightly disheartened. The reports from other returning parties did nothing to cheer us up; there were no signs. A telephone report was made to the kennels. Then the good news. Toby had found signs of three, perhaps, four pigs, about twelve miles away. It was 1030 and time for *déjeuner*.

After the harbouring, it is the custom for all those concerned to meet at some convenient inn and have breakfast; a very civilized idea. We had pork cutlets, wine, mashed potato, wine, cheese, wine and coffee.

The meet was in the gravel pit of Coulange. It was here that, with no little difficulty, my *déjeuner*-enhanced form was heaved on to my horse for the day.

There are more formalities with French hunting than there are with the British variety. At the meet, there is the *Rapport* when all the harbourers line up and make a formal presentation of what they have seen on their rounds. The Master then decides what to do on the basis of what has been reported. Toby's pigs were just across the road and that was where we went.

A brief dissertation on the French horn. The little English hunting horn has only one note. In English hunting, there are some half-dozen basic calls, and only the huntsman blows them. In France, horns are carried by a great number of people both on foot and horse. The French horn is long and curls around the body. There is a distinct call (more a little tune) for every phase of the chase, so that you can be a mile away in the forest and still know what is going on. I believe that there are something like a hundred different tunes. In addition, each hunt has its own 'fanfares' (signature tunes), and then there are tunes in honour of certain dignitaries. Sir Rupert has his own tune, *Le Jardine*.

In France, the find is called *L'Attaque*. If things go well, it is a *bonne attaque* and the alternative is a *malle attaque*. Madame was not pleased with the find. To be fair, there were four pigs all together and there was a certain amount of confusion. It is possible that the huntsman did get rather over-excited and rather overdid the operatic bits. Hounds got very divided and Madame made her feelings abundantly clear to all concerned.

A rather confused phase then followed. We found ourselves trotting hard along a ridge road apparently without benefit of sight or sound of any hounds. Cars kept appearing and producing rather excited information. There were somewhat heated councils and obviously divided opinions. As a result of one of these sessions, Madame shot off one way, and all the others shot off the other way. I know my place; I followed the Master.

We wizzed down a lane followed by a number of hard-driven cars. We stopped. We listened. Sure enough, some hounds were coming up the wood towards us. A big black-and-white hound boomed across the lane: *'C'est Téméraire: c'est bon!'* cried Madame and blew some shattering blasts on her horn.

A fluttered van screeched to a halt, two men leapt out and threw open the doors. More hounds came pouring out and were set away with Téméraire. This is the French relay system. The vans runs round behind picking up stray hounds, then nips up to the front and bungs them in at best.

Things began to settle down. More and more hounds got together. The cry was tremendous; French hounds have rather better voices than most of their English cousins. I got a good view of the boar as it ran between two woods. It looked enormous, and its apparently clumsy gait is an illusion.

We were in open country now, and keeping contact with hounds only with difficulty. The cars were doing rather better than the horses. French car followers drive with tremendous élan, and gallic enthusiasm. My wife will testify to this. She was being driven by a lady who thought that Boudicca was alive and well and living in France.

The first boar was taken after some two and a half hours. The boar will eventually stand at bay, and this is the time of maximum danger for the hounds. Several are killed every season. The boar is a formidable adversary. To prevent an accident, a responsible person has to be on the scene as quickly as possible and has to despatch the boar quickly and cleanly which is done by a thrust to the heart with a special boar spear. By the time we arrived with the horses, Toby had already 'served' the boar. I reckoned that he had done right but Madame was mortified that her guests had missed the end. Then came the news that ten hounds had been seen going on with another boar. There was some more confused riding. Enter Stanislaus (stage left) in a jeep and a great hurry. The boar was at bay. I was dragged from my horse and thrust into a van.

We arrived at a swampy thicket below the road. I would estimate that there were at least three hundred people there. I found myself being passed from hand to hand into the swamp to an accompanying chant of 'Villy, Villy (French for Willy),

Vite! Vite!' The boar was at bay in a blackthorn thicket and i
suddenly dawned on me that I was being awarded the honour
of crawling in there and despatching it. It was an interesting
moment of truth, and there were some interesting moments to
follow. However, the locals thought it to have been well done.
I was told that it was a great honour for the boar for it to
have been 'served' by an Englishman. I must confess that that
angle had not occurred to me.

That was the end of the day's hunting, but the beginning of
more pageantry. After a successful conclusion, there is always
the *Curée*. The ceremony takes place at some local house
where refreshment is dispensed. The boar is skinned and the
better joints removed for local distribution. The remains of the
carcase is then re-covered with the skin and hounds are
brought out and held up before it. The horn blowing begins.
The boar is honoured, then the hounds, the visitors, any
dignitaries present who have their own fanfare; the honour is
blown for those who 'served' the boar, the subscribers blow a
salute to the hunt staff and the hunt staff return the compliment. Then the skin is whipped away and hounds are allowed
in to their reward. The ceremony is immutable and must be
performed however late the hour and however foul the weather. It takes quite a long time.

After every hunting day, there is a dinner. That night some
fifty members of the hunt sat down at the thirteenth-century
Château du Vieux Chambord, home of Ghislain Devaulx de
Chambord. After dinner I was made to sing. Then we all sang.
The home-made pear brandy was a great song inducer.

It was a truly memorable evening to finish a day that I shall
never forget. Nor shall I forget the kindness of our hosts and
of all the people we met. They all went to immense trouble to
help us and make us welcome. I very much look forward to
going back there.

Hunting is alive and well and very much part of French
country life. Perhaps I should give the last word to the man
who, on hearing that there were no wild boar in Britain, shook
his head and said that he could not live anywhere there were
no *sangliers*: they were his life.

Chapter Twenty-One

WHEN SPRING
IS SPRUNG

SPRING IS FROWNED upon in Northumberland. All that soft southern nonsense about tweeting birds and rampant primroses is regarded with grave suspicion. Spring is something that happens to Yuppies and Barley Barons in Hampshire and has something to do with ladies with hairy legs and bare feet dancing in the dew. You certainly would not want to do much barefoot dancing up here in the spring – not unless you want all your toe nails to drop off from frost bite. Any primrose that stuck its head over the parapet would get it smartly blown off by a screaming north-easter. Spring can be a cold, dour time here and I have to admit an occasional sneaking yearning for the soft Cornish springs of my childhood; there primroses paraded unafraid and lambs gambolled in the soft sunlight instead of standing pinched and shivering in the boreal blast. I do not of course mention these yearnings locally: social ostracism would be the very least that I could expect.

So how do I know that spring has sprung? Because the curlew has arrived. I have always liked curlews. Their haunting piping is a symbol of the wild places that I love. I always look forward eagerly to hearing the first one of the season. The peewits are another welcome sign, as are the oyster catchers on the stony river bank.

There are some ruined hulks of ash trees on the farm. Someone came with a chain saw the other day and offered to 'tidy them up' (I hate chain saws), but then where would the jackdaws nest? And anyway, I think that there is altogether too much tidying up: a little scruffiness is environmentally desirable.

Another sure sign of the sap rising is mayhem amongst the cocks. I have kept duckwings for some twenty-five years (no, they are *not* bantams). If you have never seen one, they are handsome birds: golden necks and backs, blue, brown and silver on the wings, and greeny-black breasts and tails. There used to be one on the Courage Ale Label. They were originally bred as fighting cocks and whilst you and I know that cockfighting is illegal, no one has told them. They live semi-wild in and around the sheep shed.

Trouble usually arises because there are too many cocks and because Nelson the senior cock (one eye) generally appropriates eleven of the available fifteen hens for his exclusive use. Nobody messes with Nelson. This means that there are four spare hens and some seven cocks. For the last month, there has been 'stern strife and carnage drear' and dreadful scenes of rapine. I saw two cocks fighting on the back of a totally unmoved Mule ewe. The result of all this is that we are now down to four cocks and there are hens sitting everywhere. I always look forward to the first brood of the year. Game hens are marvellous mothers. Woe betide any dog that goes within spitting distance of a brood.

It snowed the other night and there were plenty of fox feetings amongst the ewes and lambs in the morning. I lost three lambs last year, but foxes have never bothered me much. I wish I could persuade a vixen to breed on the farm. On my last farm I used to have a breed of cubs every year and I never lost a lamb. I am certain that vixens never kill close to home and that they keep other intruders away. Actually, I did once lose one lamb: I found it one morning, still alive, but covered in tiny, tiny tooth marks. Such a thing had never happened before and never did again. I strongly suspect that the cubs had got up to mischief when mother was away, and I'm sure that she gave them a right seeing to when she got home.

It is, in fact, a lovely morning. I think that I shall wander down to that sheltered spot below the quarry and see if I can see a primrose. I just hope that no one round here finds out what I am doing.

Chapter Twenty-Two

THE BATTLES OF OTTERBURN

THE SIXTH HUNDREDTH anniversary of the Battle of Otterburn took place in 1988. At this point, half of you are going to say, 'You what?'; the other half are going to smile smugly and say, 'Ah yes; the Ballad of Chevy Chase.' Shame on the first lot and 'Oh no, it isn't' to the others.

In the days before rugby football was invented, the hardy borderers, both English and Scottish, used to have to keep themselves in trim by raidin', rapin' and pillagin', which cannot have been nearly such fun. Otterburn was a crucial needle match between those great protagonists: the 'Black' Douglas, and Lord Harry 'Just Call Me Hotspur' Percy.

Richard II was having domestic political problems in 1388 and so it seemed to the Scottish Earls Murray and Douglas that a nice little outing was indicated. They pillaged their way to Durham and besieged Newcastle for a bit, then sacked their way back up the Tyne and the Rede until they came to Otterburn where they stopped for a brew-up. It was here that Percy caught them. The Bishop of Durham was also trolling along some way behind with some of his chaps. Percy had three thousand men with him, whilst there were only about fifteen hundred Scots, so he probably thought that he could manage without the puffing prelate. In the July moonlight, men hewed and hacked and died until the Rede ran red with blood and the English broke and ran. Harry Percy and his brother Ralph were captured, while the Scottish triumph was tempered by the death of Douglas. I know all this because my friend Hedley (not actually him personally, you understand) got awarded a coat of arms that day for supplying some of the English horses; not that it did the English much good. I sometimes ask Hedley if the horses he hunts are left over from the Battle of Otterburn.

Chevy Chase was quite, quite different. I know that in the poem the engagement is referred to as the Battle of Otterburn, but there are major differences as you will see if you read the poem again. For one thing, it happened in the reign of Henry IV. It is much more likely that the poem refers to the battle of Homildon (1402), which took place between Wooler and the Cheviot.

This story also concerns the 'Lord Perse' (Hotspur) and the 'Doughte Douglas', but this must be another Douglas, our old friend having been already terminated with extreme prejudice at Otterburn.

Percy set out from Bamborough with the publicly declared intention of hunting deer in Douglas's 'manyre in the montaynes of Chyviat'. He took along 1500 archers which suggests that he had more in mind than a bit of quiet poaching; more a bit of Douglas baiting. At the end of the day a 'hondrith fatte hartes ther lay', but there was no sign of Douglas which caused Percy to swear a 'great othe'. However, at that moment round the corner came the man himself with 'twenty hondrith' spearmen and quite naturally wanted to know what was agoing on here then. Percy and Douglas decide to slug it out between them, but the lads were choked at being remaindered and one of them put an arrow through Douglas's 'breastbane'. Percy was proper vexed at this and leant on his sword keening a bit, whereupon he got skewered by Sir Hewe the Montgomerie, who was in turn totalled by an arrow. Meanwhile, good old Ric Witharynton had had his legs chopped off below the knees but continued to fight gamely from his stumps.

These stirring times have not been forgotten. There is going to be a week of celebration to mark the sexcentenary of the Battle of Otterburn. This will include a re-enactment of the battle by men of the Army Junior Leaders. I also hope that the English win this time; otherwise I shall be 'sikke as ye parrotte'.

Chapter Twenty-Three

EMMA

EMMA WAS A pig. She was a miserable little runt of a thing from whom her owner could foresee no viable commercial outcome. He brought her to the kennels with a view to having her written off the profit and loss account.

I looked at Jim and said that he better do it. Jim looked at me and said that really he considered it a task better undertaken by higher authority. Emma looked at both of us and squeaked. So I scratched my head and said that it really was not convenient just at that moment, and I really was in rather a hurry. Jim said, well, why not just let her run about the place for a bit? until we had the time, like; she wouldn't be any trouble; a little thing like that. So Emma joined the permanent staff.

Why Emma? I think it was because I had just been elbowed by a girl called Emma, who liked me very much but not in that way, and why could we not just be friends? The moral to this is that you should never spurn the affections of a Master of Foxhounds unless you want your name attached to some rather unflattering bit of livestock.

Emma flourished greatly. Behind every kennels is a Flesh House where the raw material is prepared before being converted into Chef's Special, or Plat du Jour. There are always certain waste products connected with this work and Emma rejoiced accordingly and waxed exceeding large.

She was a pig of great character and immense charm, always eager to greet visitors and never in the least put out if their response was not always what it might have been: as it might be leaping back into their cars and slamming the doors.

She roamed the premises at will, although I did draw the line at admitting her to my bachelor cottage. I have to say that there were those who suggested that her presence would have made very little difference to the state of the place. If hounds were out in the big grass enclosure we often used to put Emma in with them which would get her out of the way for a bit. She would play happily with them, or you would see her the centre of a group stretched out dozing in the sunshine.

Her other favourite spot was the stable yard, where again she would find a sheltered sunny spot to doze. Somewhere I have a photograph of Emma stretched out with four terriers asleep on her ample flank.

She disliked being shut up and used to make her displeasure plain by emitting a noise rather like the audience on the Wogan Show. As autumn drifted into winter and the nights became colder, we began to worry about her welfare. There was no need. Emma solved the problem herself. She used to bury herself deep in the stable muck-heap, completely out of sight in her fragrant, centrally heated hole.

There were in that country Mushroom Men. Horse manure is deemed to be great stuff for growing mushrooms and every so often a lorry would appear. Muscular Mushroom Men would fork up the contents of the muck-heap and press a few silver coins into my calloused palm for the privilege.

One frosty October morning I came, yawning and rubbing my eyes, into the stable yard in the grey light of the dawn and sleepily noted that the Mushroom Men were even then in our midst. Still yawning, and very likely having a bit of a scratch, I watched as M.M. no. 1 stepped onto the top of the muck heap and thrust his prong deep into it.

What happened next has to be considered from two separate points of view.

The first position is that of a large off-pink sow slumbering blamelessly in warm and scented darkness into whose rear end is stuck a four-pronged fork.

The second position to be considered is that of a hard-working Mushroom Man in whose belly last night's ale is still curdling and whose head is still ringing with the effects of said ale and his wife's forthright comments on the matter.

If you are the aforesaid pig, you proclaim your hurt fortissima and emerge from the heap like a polaris missile.

If you are a crapulous Mushroom Man standing on a screaming and exploding muck heap, you go six feet straight in the air and then, gibbering the while, curve gracefully into the bramble thicket behind.

Oh dear, oh dear, it was a horrid scene. Bacon and mushrooms anyone?

Chapter Twenty-Four

THE ART
OF WHISTLING

How is your whistle? Perhaps whistling is not as big in your life as it is in mine. For one thing, whistling is the main method of communicating with a distant collie dog. I am sure that a lot of you have watched *One Man and His Dog* on the box and have been amazed by the way that the dogs respond to their handler's whistling. You see the top end of the trade on these occasions. There are many layers of coarse dog handling when you get below the top flight. There are those who say that trial dogs are overtrained, that they will only move to a whistle and that they have had the ability to think for themselves trained and bred out of them. That is Controversy with a capital C and I am not going to be mug enough to get embrangled in that one.

However, there is no doubt that whistling is valuable. A whistle carries farther and penetrates a dog's consciousness when a lot of increasingly incoherent bellowing may fail. There are three basic commands for a collie:

'Come by': go round the sheep in a clockwise direction.

'Away to me': go round the sheep in an anti-clockwise direction.

'Lay doon': stop.

There can be complications in that in some parts of the country 'Come by' and 'Away' are used the other way about. It is better to buy a dog whose clock goes the same way as yours does. There are other complications. I once bought a dog who had been worked in Welsh, and we suffered a mutual crisis of incomprehension. I got a kind Welsh-speaking friend to teach me some elementary commands, which seemed to work very well. It was not until long afterwards that another

kind Welsh-speaking friend told me that the clock-wise command that I had been using in fact meant: 'Go you and
defecate in the little green valley'; the others were nothing like
as delicate. It was then much too late to change and, anyway,
there are not many Welsh speakers in the north of England.

The voice commands all have an equivalent whistle. The
basic 'stop' is a long drawn out declining note at which a well-
trained dog will drop in its tracks – (For Sale. Collie Dog.
Twelve months. Just started to run. Stops to whistle.) Old
Gow taught me a lot of my dog handling. He explained the
whistle commands as 'pupPY' for clockwise, and 'EEyore' for
anti-clockwise. I understood exactly what he meant and if I can
then, so can you. It is a two-note job, of course.

There are all sorts of subsidiary whistle commands: such as
'walk on and take the sheep away up the hill whilst I lean on
my stick down here and light my pipe'; or 'Now that you are
up at the top of the hill, bring those sheep down to where I
am leaning on my stick and smoking my pipe.' I have been
trying to devise one for 'Cut away home now and tell mother
to put the kettle on', but we have not got there; yet.

All this is all very fine and dandy, but how do you produce
these whistles? The very fortunate have their front teeth so
disposed that they can produce a noise like the Cornish
Riviera Express going through Bodmin Road station. Then
there are those who can split an ear at 100 yards with two
fingers stuck in the mouth. There are times when the required
fingers may just have been intimately concerned with such
esoteric tasks as removing the soiled wool from around a
ewe's rear echelons. I have never acquired the knack of
whistling through my fingers; or the taste.

I have a whistle. Take a piece of tin. Cut an oval about two
inches long by one and a half across. Fold it in two so that the
two sides are about 1/16th of an inch apart. Drill a hole through
the middle. Insert in mouth on top of tongue. You will now be
able to shame the blackbird. But do have it anchored round
your neck with a piece of string; I do not want to have to come
round and fish it out of the back of your throat with my fingers.

Chapter Twenty-Five

KENNING AND COUNTING

IN THE DAYS WHEN when I was at the height of my majesty and power, sitting at the meet amongst my hounds and looking rather like a pre-Telecom telephone kiosk on a horse, people would come up to me and ask me whether I knew all my hounds by name. My response to this was always to ask the lady (it was always a lady) whether she knew the names of all her children. Persistent ladies (and such things are not uncommon) would then say, yes, of course, but that is quite different because hounds all look the same. I would then have to point out that to the general public her children all looked the same, and uniformly ghastly at that. This would usually close the conversation.

To an untrained eye, a pack of hounds is just a mass of hounds. To those who know and love them, hounds are as individual as children. Not only do you know their names but their characters and personalities, their strengths and weaknesses. To know each individual is not as difficult as people might think, especially when you are amongst them every day; after all, you have known not only them but their parents, grandparents, and fore-elders for many generations.

It is a bit more difficult when you take over a fresh pack of hounds. I used to reckon that it would take me a month to learn the names of say forty couple of hounds. Mind you, there are certain packs where the learning must be a nightmare. The Belvoir hounds, for instance, are all black and tan, whilst the Curre hounds are (or used to be) uniformly lemon and white. A lot will depend on how good a 'kenner' you are.

Some hound- and stockmen have fantastic memories for the animals they have known; they 'ken them weel'. I know a man who took on a kennel with over sixty couples of hounds in it and he had their names off pat in one week. I know another man to whom I showed a hound once and who exactly remembered that hound five years later.

You would think, and I would agree with you, that kenning would be even more difficult with sheep. I look at my small flock twice a day, but I am a poor kenner. I would probably recognize a strange sheep amongst mine, and I think I might be able to pick one of mine out of another flock of similar sheep. Mind you, there are always certain individuals who stick out. There is Old Daisy who has her tenth crop of twins running with her. Old Hirple had a broken leg once over. There is the ewe with the magpie face who nearly died of pneumonia, and Lucy who always butts me in the bum in hope of a mint, but I do not really ken the majority.

Fred who does occasional work for me knows them much better than I do. He will immediately recognize such and such a sheep as the 'auld bitch' who was in the pen at the bottom of the passage last lambing. 'Yon white-faced youth' was the one who had a big dead lamb and we set another pair on her. I would not begin to remember such detail, but there are men herding 600 ewes who will ken them as well as a huntsman kens his hounds.

Counting is another art. Try counting a flock of sheep or a pack of hounds next time you see one. A skilled man will look at a moving mass and know instinctively if it is short of the required number. I remember a man telling me that he went to look at some sheep with a shepherd friend. As they drove along the valley bottom, they could see the long lines of sheep coming down the fell to the farm. The shepherd watched them as they drove along. As they approached the farm he said, 'Fifteen hundred and forty.' He was wrong – by three.

It is necessary to concentrate when counting sheep; slacken off for a second and you can lose the count. I have always felt very sorry for the chap who had got to 2,347 when the collie widdled into his boot.

Chapter Twenty-Six

THE ARMY
AS TRUSTEES

To the Otterburn Ranges: one of 'a thirty-strong group of local authority representatives and conservation specialists'. I am not quite sure in which category I came and neither was anybody else – but they all stared at me in horror and asked what on earth I was doing there. I was there because I had been invited but that did not really seem to satisfy anybody. I quite expected men with blackened faces to abseil down the central heating duct and put a bag over my head. They gave me rather a good cup of coffee instead.

The object of the exercise was public relations. The Army is a major landowner (58,000 acres at Otterburn alone) in some very beautiful parts of Britain. There is chuntering amongst certain citizens because civilian access to these wild places is somewhat curtailed. It seems a very simple equation to me. An army must train if it is to be efficient. An inefficient army would be a waste of taxpayers' money. Military training must entail lots of flashing and banging which is best done in the wide open spaces; there is quite enough of that sort of thing in urban areas as it is. Nor can you have multiple family units eating al fresco meals all over the target area. A picnic rocketed by the massed airforces of NATO is a spoilt picnic and if the Belgian Special Forces were to get mixed up with the cucumber sandwiches, well, the results would be too terrible to even think about. However, the Army was at pains to point out that normal life did exist on the ranges.

The Otterburn Ranges are not just a waste of shell-holes, they are are a living workplace. There are thirty-one tenanted farms on the range and some 50,000 sheep at peak times. Many families have farmed on the ranges since before the Army first acquired land there in 1911.

There is no doubt that farming on a live firing range may require a different routine: the herding has to be done early in the morning and late at night. It is a rhythm that people learn to work with, and the strains imposed by the landlord's requirements are reflected in the rents. Problems do arise, of course. Local folklore always blames the Belgians when sheep disappear — but when it comes to sheep one should always keep the reputation of the Bogshire Fusiliers in mind. My impression is that there is a very good system for dealing with problems, and a good relationship between landlord and tenant. I would not mind farming an army farm (Property Services Agency please note).

There is another important point. Had it not been for the Army, all those farms and all those lovely wild hills would have been smothered in ghastly conifers when successive governments succumbed to forest mania in the Forties and Fifties. In this connection, it is encouraging to hear that the Army has a plan for regenerating broadleaved woodlands on the range. They have recently acquired 2,500 acres of Sitka spruce which will be replaced with native hardwoods.

We had a guided tour of points of interest in a fleet of coaches. The only thing that the Army organization had fallen down on was the weather: a sullen North Sea fret persisted all day. The TV cameras were made so desperate by lack of a view that they were even reduced to filming me at one stage: not that they could have done better anyway.

This bit of ground, between the Rivers Coquet and Rede, was a real hot spot in the days of the border raids. The remains of the bastles (fortified farmhouses) are still scattered about the hills. Many were recycled into newer houses over the years, but some have survived and there are restoration plans in hand. The bastle was a two-storey job: a big vaulted chamber on the ground floor and an upstairs room. When the hairy Scots came whooping over the hill, you shoved all the stock into the ground floor room, and nipped up through a trap door with the wife and the weans. There you stayed until the Scots had got back into the chara and gone on elsewhere, leaving the ground littered with export lager cans, no doubt.

I thoroughly enjoyed my day. Most people want to see the hills and wild places protected, but they must remain places where people live and work. The Army is doing a good job of keeping its bit of hill alive and productive. I think that they are good trustees of the hills.

'See you, Jimmie!'

Chapter Twenty-Seven

FIELDSPORTSPERSONS
AT THE GAME FAIR

WHAT IS A GAME FAIR? It is a jamboree of Field Sports with the emphasis on shooting and fishing. There are various minor variations that take place about the country, but *the* Game Fair is always understood to be the one run by the Country Landowners' Association. This takes place at a different stately home every year, and this year (1988) the short straw was drawn by the Duke of Roxburghe. The Duke hangs his coronet at Floors Castle near Kelso in the Borders. It is a magnificent setting on the banks of the Tweed. The received wisdom is that it is a magnificent house which Sir Walter Scott described as 'altogether a kingdom for Oberon and Titania to dwell in'. That is as maybe. To me it looks like a giant baroque jelly mould. If it had been mine, I would have knocked it down long ago and built something comfortable instead.

Somebody asked me what the theme for this year's Game Fair would be. I can now tell you: it will be MUD. An inch of rain fell on the site over Thursday night and Friday morning. I arrived at 0700 on Friday morning and they were already towing cars *in*. By the time I left at 1200, the whole site seemed to be listing badly to starboard. Over 100,000 punters are expected during the weekend.

Fieldsportspersons are pretty much inured to the rigours of the British climate and there was some jolly Dunkirk spirit abroad amongst the bacon butties in the early morning car park.

The trade stands are a great feature of the Game Fair. There is Gun Dealers' Row where you can buy guns. There is Fishermen's Row where piscatorial desires may be satisfied. There is Gamekeepers' Row, where they presumably sell gamekeepers. In fact, you can buy almost anything that a normal healthy person would require from the stands.

The Boy and I went and did our shopping early; indeed many of the stands were not yet open. The pictures and fine arts people were noticeably slothful. The vintners had just started to appear, standing outside their booths yawning and scratching themselves intimately. However, we managed to purchase two Cecil Aldin prints, a mega dog bed for the Rottweiler, a wind speed indicator, a deerstalker hat to stop the rain dripping down my neck, a widget for cleaning muddy boots, and a packet of strong mints: how is that for eclecticism?

One sees a lot of people as one mooches about. In a recent copy of a sporting magazine, there was a photograph of me wearing nothing but a straw hat and a pair of socks. It was amazing how many people recognized me with my clothes on.

There are numerous exhibitions and demonstrations: sheep-dog displays, falcon flying, Pipes and Drums of the Royal Scots Dragoon Guards, parade of hounds, and gun dog training to name but a few.

I watched a sheep dog display. The sheep were not being at all obliging, and we could not but admire the calm efficiency of dogs and handler. The Boy said that it was a bit different to the coarse dog handling practised at home.

We did not see the hawks in action but admired them on their stand. I had never heard of a Ferruginous buzzard before and I had to look up the word. It simply means that the Buzzard was rusty.

There are all-day fishing demonstrations and there was going to be a chance to have a go at catching a salmon on the Lower Floors beat on the famous Tweed. The Tweed was a chocolate-coloured torrent which would have yielded no greater piscatorial prize than the odd derelict oil drum or a passing dead sheep.

By mid morning, the walkways were hock deep, even tractors were getting stuck, and people of small stature were being advised to travel in groups. My heart went out to the man who was trying to sweep the mud from the front of his stand with a little house brush: I wonder if he was called Partington.

We left the fair at noon and passed mile upon mile of cars queuing to get in. As we came away, there was a man offering helicopter trips for a tenner. The Boy reckoned that if all the people got in then that might be their only way out.

Coarse dog-handler

Chapter Twenty-Eight

STRIKEBOUND IN LE HAVRE

DURING HOT SUMMER days, I often think about polo ponies. You must understand I do not play polo. Even if I could afford the vast expense (which I cannot), I am more or less incapable of hitting a ball when both I and it are stationary. Anyway, there are better things to do with a galloping horse.

Some years ago I met this chap in a pub. He wanted someone to drive him and a lorry to central France to collect four polo ponies. As I could not afford a holiday that year, it seemed like a good idea.

It was agreed that the outward leg should include a night in Paris for 'spiritual and cultural refreshment'.

I do not know what vehicle you were driving on the first occasion that you encountered the rush hour traffic on the Paris Périphérique, but I am here to tell you that a TK Bedford cattle wagon is as good as any. To French drivers 'might is right'.

My companion claimed to know a 'smashing little hotel' just off the Place St Germain. However, crafty Johnny Crapaud had moved the Place St Germain since his last visit: probably something to do with the Common Market.

'Let's ask this chappy,' he said and somehow he had the wit to find a person whose basic English managed to match our basic French.

'Ze Place St Germain ees a nerty place,' the Frenchman said and, in case we had missed the point, reinforced his message with unmistakable sign language. 'I sher yew,' and he hopped up onto the step, gave the 'finger' to all the solid citizens protesting at the hold up and off we went.

It is one thing to drive a lorry in Paris, but quite another thing to park it. The sign beside the lorry said '*Stationnement interdit*'. Our new friend shrugged: '*C'est seulement un peu interdit*,' he said.

I am quite certain that you do not want to hear about Poole in Paris; in fact I think that we should now cut to the bit where our intrepid travellers arrive on the docks at Le Havre, tired and hot, with four polo ponies (also tired and hot) but just nicely in time to clear customs and catch the Friday afternoon boat.

The customs officer we copped for was a Senegalese Marxist. His face lit up when he found what the consignment was.

'*Non!*' he said. The documentation was all wrong. Clearance was refused. I should explain that it was the start of a bank holiday and the French seamen were due to go on strike at midnight. We dug out a French shipping agent who was packing his bucket and spade. He shrugged. The papers were *un peu* incorrect, but normally, it would only be a little problem . . . However, he regretted that the town administration had just been taken over by the Communists, the chief officer was a Communist; polo ponies et puff, puff.

'I'll just scoot back to England and get it sorted,' said my companion.

What do you do on a strike-bound French dock with four weary horses? You hope something nice will happen.

What may actually happen is that a boy on a racing bicycle appears whilst you are watering the horses, and speaks perfect English. What may then happen is that the entire local riding club (which just happens to be run by the ex-Mayor recently ousted by the Communists) descends upon you and removes you and the horses.

I will not bore you with details of the weekend because, to be honest, they have never been entirely clear to me. It is probably best that the hazy images that remain stay hazy.

On the Tuesday, the seamen returned to work and my companion returned with documentation so impressive that even our favourite customs officer was unable to fault it, although it was not for want of trying. He was so upset at losing us that he followed the lorry all the way to the boat.

After it was stowed we went on deck and leant on the taffrail and blow me down if the wretched fellow was not still there, glaring. We waited until the ferry was cast off and there was clear water between us and the dock, then we both leant over the rail and gave him a comprehensive sailor's farewell. He screamed, threw his hat on the ground and started jumping on it. It was the first time that I had ever seen someone actually do that except in the *Beano*.

Chapter Twenty-Nine

TO HORSE, TO HORSE

AUGUST IS THE TIME of year when people tend to buy horses. The point has been made that most of the problems in life can be traced to three causes: Women, Horses and Motor Vehicles: discuss.

There are four sources from which you can buy horses: from a friend, from an advertisement, at an auction sale, and from your Friendly Neighbourhood Dealer. In all cases the Emptor should jolly well Caveat. There is no honour in horse dealing, and Pillars of Church, State and Society will stick you over a horse and pocket your money. They will do you with a song in their heart and without so much as a minor eructation from their conscience.

Do not buy a horse from a friend, if you wish that friendship to maintain.

Advertisements are usually a snare and a delusion. You may drive many weary and fruitless miles following up advertisements. Let us suppose that you require a nice quality heavyweight hunter; perfect gentleman; perform across any country; quiet to clip, shoe and box. There is a horse advertised that might just be the answer to your prayer. You telephone the owner (sounds *really nice*), who tells you that his/her horse is just what you want. You drive 150 miles, and find a washy-looking runt that might have one sound leg out of the four. The advertiser works on the principle that he can lose nothing by getting you to come and look, that you might just be stupid enough to bite, and anyway he will be drinking his tea in front of the telly whilst you are driving home in a sulk and a motorway queue.

If a horse is any good, then it is unlikely ever to appear at auction. I have used auction sales to sell horses that I wished to get out of sight and mind. I had a horse in an auction once: people were looking at it, and I was struggling because I am a rotten liar. Up came a dealer of my acquaintance who owed me a favour: he sized up the situation, and took over. He was a fine upstanding man, of commanding appearance, and with a piercing blue eye with which he fixed all enquirers. I stood by, with quaking soul, whilst this man, who had never seen the horse before, sang of its virtues, its kindness, its love of widows and orphans, its amazing abilities: only for sale because the Capting (this was me, whose offer of service Her Majesty had once roundly rejected) had suddenly been sent abroad to defend his country . . . It was a great performance, and it sold the horse – but you see what I mean about auctions.

This brings us neatly to dealers. You will like horse dealers. They are men of great charm and presence. They will give you tea and whisky. They will convulse you with their wit and humour. Their gaze will unflinchingly meet yours.

It goes without saying that they have in their yard the very horse that you are looking for. The horse is always 'just over from Ireland', and has always carried the Master of the famous Tullaghmore Hunt (how many good horses this happy man must ride). You should discard any unworthy suspicion that you saw the very same horse somewhere in the last paragraph. In fact His Lordship was in the yard only this morning, wasn't he, Fred? (Very true, sir; very true), and just about had the horse bought. *But*, seeing as how it's you, and how it is obvious that you and the horse are made for each other. Didn't I say that, Fred, as soon as the gentleman walked into the yard . . .

I hope that you will appreciate, by now, that if you are set on trouble, then Women and Motor Vehicles may well work out cheaper.

Chapter Thirty

THE GREAT DRIVE

Not an August passes but that I remember the Great Cattle Drive.

When I was young and slim, and my moustache was newly bloomed, I lived in Devon, on the southern edge of Dartmoor. A neighbour telephoned me one day: he had just brought three hundred Galloway cows and their attendant calves out of the deepest recesses of the moor, and he wanted some help to move them about four miles, to the fields which were to be their home for the time being. He would provide the ponies; all that I had to do was to present myself on Gibbet Down at first light the next morning, and we would have them through the village, 'up the Main', and safely tucked away before the first sign of traffic.

There are certain things that now need to be put in perspective. Galloways are tough, hardy and hairy – and their hairiness is not only physical.

The 'Main', hereinbefore referred to, was the A38 Plymouth-Exeter road, in its old, twisting, pre dual carriageway form; a main artery for holiday traffic (then, as now) and the month was August.

Back to Gibbet Down: an evocative scene in the grey light of dawn: milling, bellowing cattle, and we trailhands slouched in our saddles, and making the noises that we had all learnt from watching *Rawhide* on the telly (B & W). The track down to the village lay through a picturesque hanging oakwood that dropped steeply to the river below. The first problem arose here. The field where the cows had been held over night lacked water. The herd was thirsty. As soon as the gate was opened, the whole lot disappeared into the greenwood, with many a crash and a bellow, heading for the water that they could smell below. I have already suggested that Galloways tend to be highly strung, and this lot were wild as fitch ferrets. It is sufficient to say that it took us four hours to extract them from the wood. It was just nicely nine o'clock when we were through the village and onto the 'Main': the heat and the traffic were just starting to increase.

The Devon roads were never built with traffic flow in mind: they are bounded with high earth banks and there are no verges. It does not take many cows to fill a Devon road: three hundred cows, plus calves, fill an awful lot of road, very comprehensively. As the heat increased, the pace got slower and slower.

Denzil and I were on duty at the rear, and this brought us into continuous contact with the travelling holidaymakers. I regret to say that some of our followers rapidly became querulous. Denzil handled the public relations side. He was well qualified for the work, being nearly seven feet tall, big for his age, and covered in matted black hair: to all entreaties as to how far we were going, he would growl, 'Lunnon', and go back to being at peace with his pipe.

It was two and a half hours before we turned off the road, and I have to admit that no car had passed in all that time. We got the cows in their field, and were standing about mopping our brows and mentally murdering pints, when the police car arrived. I have never seen two such hot, and angry, policemen. Were we aware that we had created a solid block of standing, steaming, melting, traffic right back to Plymouth (11 miles)? Was there any reason why we should not be clapped in irons, put to the question, flogged, incarcerated, and the key flung into Plymouth Sound? We lesser mortals started taking cover behind our ponies, but the Leader was made of sterner stuff. He pointed out that if we were arrested then the ponies would have to come too. I suspect that the constables had had a trying enough day without having to explain to the sergeant what all those ponies were doing, eating the Wanted posters, and otherwise marking their presence in his nice clean station. We got our pints after all.

Chapter Thirty-One

THE WEDDING OF
THE YEAR

I WENT TO A WEDDING recently. So what? I hear you say, nothing special in that. I expect that most of you spend your whole time dashing from church to church with a penguin suit and a box of tissues. I do not like weddings. Weddings mean the disruption of my domestic routine, the squeezing of myself into a suit that is totally anachronistic in relation to my present bulk, melting slowly in the heat and drinking what seems to be warm paint stripper. Therefore I avoid weddings.

This one was different. The two main participants were (and are, I hope) old and valued friends whose romance I had watched from afar with avuncular interest. Also, I had been cast with a minor speaking role. The happy couple had come upon me at a moment of repose. My pipe was drawing nicely, there was a well-earned whisky in my paw, I was at peace with the world. Of course I would say a few words at their wedding. Only when they had gone did the full horror of what I had agreed to do dawn upon me.

The day started badly. It was hot; two lots of sheep got muddled up and had to be sorted; the house was full of people from afar; I still had not polished my speech; and it was hot. By the time we joined the queue of cars in the narrow road to the church, I was in very tatty fettle indeed.

There was a guard of honour from a certain well-known Knightsbridge regiment standing to attention on either side of the church door. I felt that I ought to inspect them. My wife lead me away by the ear. She does rather a lot of that.

It is a nice little church. The seating allocation was six persons per pew which was fine except for the fact that I sit for two: if we had been sheep, they would have had the cruelty man in, but at least sheep do not wear morning coats. It was very very hot. The only thing that saved me was that the wedding race-cards were stiff and I was able to fan myself.

It was a good old-fashioned service with all the hymns one used to sing in College Chapel before the Church of England became all guitars and sandals. As I could remember most of the words I was able to sing and fan at the same time.

It would be a cliché to say that the bride looked lovely: all brides look lovely, but this one has a bit of a head start.

Back at the ranch, I was actually beginning to enjoy myself. I had found a nice bosky corner where the ladies with the bottles came with pleasing regularity. There was a nice tree to lean against. Several jolly men came and poked me in the tummy and said how fat I was getting (pot and kettle to them) and several lovely ladies came and kissed me. This was very pleasing but much complicated because of the frightful hats they all insisted on wearing which either poked me in the eye or made me sneeze.

My mood melted along with my collar.

I was content.

A fluttered son of the family appeared: The Speech, The Speech. I was late: where was I? why was I? I was passed through the crowd rather as happens when one dances 'The Drops of Brandy' ('Strip the Willow' to most of you). The bride stamped her lovely foot at me and the butler gave me a rollocking before announcing me. What of the speech? The only good thing about it was that it lasted only 3.5 minutes.

That night there was a dance which was very jolly. I am not a dancer but I was happy watching the young cavort.

I felt that it had been a great and happy day that I had enjoyed in spite of myself. I also felt that the day had been a little piece of social history. This day there had gathered together Lords of the Land and Tractor Drivers; Knacker Men and High Sheriffs. The local newspaper called it 'the county wedding of the year' which is almost certainly true but, more than that, it was also a celebration of the social cohesion of Rural England, the Old England.

Chapter Thirty-Two

WOOD HUSBANDRY

THE SURGEONS CAME last Saturday. Perhaps I should hasten to add that they were tree surgeons.

There are two woods on the farm. One of them is a long shelter belt of Sitka spruce. It was planted in the fifties when Sitka was the forester's buzz word. They are undoubtedly hardy and thrifty trees. You only have to see how they survive on bleak hillsides which were once only good for grouse and sheep. The fact that many of these plantings were only made financially possible by liberal inputs of taxpayer's hard-earned gelt is neither here nor there. We should also gloss over the fact that the cost of extracting the timber from many of these plantations will nicely wipe out any putative income. I do not like Sitka spruce: its plantations are dark, gloomy and dreary and I wish that it had stayed in Sitka (wherever that may be). However, I have to admit that it does make a good shelter belt. I built my house on the west side of our shelter belt. All our really nasty weather comes out of the south-east, from the Urals via the North Sea: very little glasnost in the Russian weather.

Last year it occurred to me that by the time I am creaking about in my sixties, the Sitka will be ready to fell and what will then temper the wind to the arthritic Poole? So I am planting another shelter belt to the east of the existing one. This one is going to be a mixed plantation with more emphasis on broadleaved trees since this will allow some ground cover to develop as well. The ground under the existing Sitka plantation is dead and dark and no birds sing.

The other bit of farm woodland is a tiny copse that sticks out into the village like a ——; well, it sticks out anyway. The copse has been neglected and many of the trees are miles past their best, including some elms which are very dead and in the shadow of which new houses have been built.

I found a chap to come and deal with them, and he took the trees out of the middle of the copse. He then looked at the elms, scratched his chin and went to look for a winch. That was a year ago.

So the tree surgeons came. There were four of them, a cheerful bunch and immensely professional. I would not do their job for much fine gold. I get vertigo on a domestic step ladder. I am also terrified of chain saws. I would be even more terrified sixty foot up a tree. Because, you see, they take down the difficult trees, piece by piece, from the top. They climb without apparent effort with the aid of climbing irons and canvas webbing. In case you have never seen climbing irons (and I had not) they are long steel spikes strapped on to the lower leg, so that the spike digs into the tree trunk and stops the climber sliding down. With these and a webbing waist harness a man can 'stand' on a vertical trunk and have both hands free to operate his saw which, when not in use, hangs below him on a long line. In this way, and with cunningly rigged ropes to make sure that everything falls where it should (not through Mr Bells' garage roof, for instance), the tree is brought to stump level.

Other trees can be dropped in one by skilful use of a hydraulic winch.

It was fascinating to watch and I spent much more time down there than I should. I have, however, learned a lot. I did not know that elm and beech are the two heaviest woods. Whilst elm rots in the middle, the outer wood is extremely dense and water-resistant. Because of this, the Romans used hollowed-out elm for drains.

One of the reasons I do not like chain saws is that I once saw a man cut halfway through his thigh. The surgeons would have had little sympathy for him. They say that anyone who uses a chain saw without protective clothing is several kinds of fool. They wore special gloves and trousers whose padding would stop a moving chain. They also wore special boots and had helmets with face-guards and ear-protectors. So if you are thinking of doing a little gentle chainsawing in your shorts and shirt, think on a bit. Follow the example of the professionals and cover up, otherwise you may need the services of another kind of surgeon – or even of the elm, whose other name is 'the Coffin Tree'.

Chapter Thirty-Three

THE
ENGLISH CONNECTION
AT CHANTILLY

W HAT DO MARÉCHAL FOCH, Général Le Clerc and Charles
Pratt have in common? The answer is that they all have
roads named after them in and around Chantilly.

The first two were obviously military gentlemen of credit
and renown but what of Charles Pratt? He was an English
trainer of racehorses who operated from Chantilly between
1872 and 1914. His eminence may serve to emphasize the
strong English influence in this centre of French racing. The
links are still strong and still valued.

It was to investigate these links that our little task force set
out. It consisted of Mr Kenneth Mason, photographer extraordinary; my wife who considers that an innocent like me
would only get into trouble with foreign parts (?) and, anyway,
she was due for a break and, anyway, she would do the
driving. This she did very well in spite of a marked tendency
to stop suddenly athwart four lines of French traffic and start
screaming. The last member of the party was me.

I think that we should start the story in proper style with
Princes and a Castle.

The estates of Chantilly were owned by the Princes of
Condé. The famous 'Grand' Condé built the existing pile
which is straight out of a fairy tale, enturreted and bemoated;
full of rich and beautiful tapestries and lots of pictures of
plump ladies wearing languorous poses, cherubs and not much
else. It is certainly a place of wonder and delight to any
visitor, but I should not think much fun to live in. *Noblesse
oblige* can be a draughty concept.

The 'Grand's' grandson was absolutely potty on hunting and he built Les Grandes Écuries (the Great Stables) of which more anon. It should be said that his intentions when building this quite extraordinary edifice were not entirely worldly. He was convinced that he was going to return to this mortal coil in equine form and wanted to ensure that he would continue to live in the style to which he had been accustomed.

He also laid out the forest in its present form with dead straight rides intersecting at roundabouts, rather like a spider's web.

In 1886 the whole estate was willed to the Institut de France (a body of academicians) who are the present proprietors.

What, I hear you say, has all this to do with racehorses? Be patient, I beg of you. The background is important because, but for the Bourbons and the Institut, the forest might have become charcoal and blocks of flats; there would be nowhere for horses to train and Chantilly would not be able to call itself the 'City of Horses'.

When he could spare the time from hunting, the Grand-Stable-Prince also liked a bit of racing. The broad stretch of ground in front of the castle and the stables was an ideal spot for that bit of racing – and there the 'Hippodrome' of Chantilly stands to this day.

Today Chantilly has the biggest concentration of racehorses in the world. Remain seated 'Disgusted, Newmarket': do not reach for your pen yet: you have 2300 horses in training; Chantilly has 3200 (or trois mille, deux cent, if you prefer it). The point of all this is (always supposing that there is one) that Chantilly is what it is today because of the English, and especially the Newmarket, Connection.

In the latter part of the last century there was a great migration of English to Chantilly: trainers, jockeys, stable lads. A great tradition was started that maintains to this day and some notable dynasties were also founded: Head, Cunnington, Bartholomew to name but a few and the third, fourth and fifth generations still live and train in Chantilly to this day. Nor has the process finished. Although most of the jockeys and lads are now French, English trainers still set up at Chantilly and carry on the great tradition.

Charlie Milbank has trained in Chantilly for over twenty years, arriving there from Yorkshire by the slightly roundabout route of New Zealand, Ireland and USA. Jonathan Hammond has only been in Chantilly for five or so years; he has already achieved success and recognition as a trainer. He originally came out as assistant trainer to M. Fabre. He now has seventy-five horses in his charge and is negotiating to take on another yard.

My first problem was how to find all the right people.

Always go to the top: that is what I reckon. The Top in Chantilly is La Société d'Encouragement pour l'Amélioration des Races de Chevaux en France; or to give it its slightly more snappy demotic title La Société d'Encouragement. The Chantilly Director is M. Christian de Lagarde and the Director of Public Relations is M. Marcel Riou: two neater encapsulations of Gallic dynamism, drive and élan you will never meet. Their immediate response to any request was *'pas de probleme'*. Did M. Mason wish to photograph a horse in front of the Château? It had never been allowed before, but *pas de probleme*. Did we wish to go here? did we wish to come there? did we wish to meet such a person? were the gates of a certain place closed? *Pas de probleme*: the telephone was picked up, the magic words 'Société d'Encouragement' were uttered and suddenly all paths were made smooth and broad.

On day one, 0645 found us shivering in the fog on Les Aigles. This is 550 acres of turf and sand gallops and exercise tracks owned by the Société, the beauty of which we were later to appreciate. At that time all we could see was the sudden loom of galloping horses in the fog.

Then 0800 found us at the racecourse which was open for training that day (racing at Chantilly only happens in June). The fog had lifted a bit. Enough for me to wonder yet again how on earth flat race jockeys ever manage to stay on a horse with their knees cocked up under their chins. This reverie was broken by meeting M. John Cunnington, the famous trainer, fourth generation from the original Cunnington who had come over as King Louis Phillipe's coachman.

It was now time for a spot of *petit déjeuner* which seemed

like a good idea, but not before the rather frustrated Mr Mason had insisted on taking a very unfortunate picture of me on the weighing-room scales. M. Riou closed his eyes when the needle went round for the fourth time.

It was still foggy as we drank our coffee with M. de Lagarde. Would we get the photograph at the Château? M. de Largarde said something irritable into his walkie-talkie and the sun immediately came out.

The Château was closed to the public so the attendant gendarmes had no one to shoo away. However, there was a large van parked in the wrong place: something to do with a film they were making inside. After a certain amount of chat to and fro, a sulky looking youth in powdered wig and knee breeches (that sort of film) with a dog-end stuck to his lower lip came and moved it.

In the afternoon we went to the Grandes Écuries. The building was closed to the public, but *'pas de probleme'*.

The Great Stables are just that. The main stable block is 610 feet long, 36 feet wide (interior), and 91 feet high; the walls are 13 feet thick. There was accommodation for 240 horses. Behind the main stables were the coach houses, outdoor school and kennels for 250 couple of hounds. This quite extraordinary building was quietly crumbling until, in 1982, M. Yves Bienaimé came to an agreement with the Institut. Since then he has begun to restore the building at his own expense and has turned it into what he calls a Live Equestrian Museum showing the history and developement of the horse through the ages and in all its degrees. Displays of equitation are also held there.

M. Bienaime gave us a personal tour of what he describes as his 'grand passion'. Such an undertaking must indeed require a very great passion and not inconsiderable expense. You should not miss a chance to visit M. Bienaime's passion and for a modest £8000 you can mount a cocktail party for twelve hundred of your friends there (equestrian display included). Ideal for your next office party.

Hunting is still an important part of the Chantilly scene. The forest is hunted by the Hunt of the Three Forests and in the late afternoon we went to the kennels under the stern eye of the great Madame D'Aillières, the Master, to watch hounds having their *Soupe*. At one time, it looked as though Mr Mason's photographic enthusiasm might get him included on the menu.

I must now talk about the forest. The Forest of Chantilly is a place of great beauty and tranquillity. The vast oaks and beeches form a vaulting for the long straight rides. The rides themselves are sand and those used for training are raked continuously throughout the training period by M. de Lagarde's tractors and harrows.

The early morning sun shafts down through the trees. A jay calls. A red squirrel dashes across the ride. Between the trees there are glimpses of strings of horses snaking through the forest.

'*Attention!*' says the guard who controls people crossing the gallops. I am not a racing man, neither am I really a horse man within the meaning of the act, but a man must indeed be mean of soul if he can fail to be stirred by the sight of a galloping thoroughbred horse. To watch a string of seventy pass by one after the other is deeply impressive. Every morning whilst we were at Chantilly, we went either to Les Aigles or to the forest (sometimes both) and each morning was different, fascinating and exciting.

Our researches into the English Connection were ceaseless. Early in the morning or late of the night, it was all the same to our tireless little band; never once did our steps slacken on the path of duty. Thus we came to Mme. Griff.

Mme. Laura Griff is married to a Frenchman and is the *patronne* of the Tipperary Restaurant. The Tipperary is famous for its cartoons of Chantilly characters. These were done in the last century by M. Bisetzky who was also the station master, a magician, a composer, a flautist and a man of letters. Everyone decided that the cartoon of the Duc de Hamilton riding on an elephant (he was a well-built chap) looked just like me, so they sat me down where the Aga Khan usually sits, and gave me one of the truly memorable meals of my sheltered life. It was a good thing that it was in the line of duty; otherwise I might have been accused of gluttony.

It was a truly fascinating visit. I did not really know what to expect when I went to the 'City of Horses', but whatever I expected, it was surpassed. I shall remember it as a place of great traditions allied to all that is best in progressive techniques. I shall remember the magnificent stable yards and lovely buildings. I shall certainly remember the kindness and hospitality. Most of all I shall remember the forest in the early morning, with galloping horses looming out of the mist. The English Connection is alive and well in Chantilly and I am glad to have been part of it.

He closed his eyes when the needle went round for the fourth time

Chapter Thirty-Four

SPARKLING CIDER HORSES

FOR THE FIRST TIME in thirty years I am not in possession of a horse. My feelings are a mixture of regret, for great times past, and relief, because I shall never have to pretend to be brave again.

My relationship with the horse has been a somewhat uneasy one. Good horsemen are born and can then be polished into gems of equitation. You cannot turn a rough-hewn flint into a gem however hard you polish, and 'flintlike' would be a very fair description of my horsemanship. I was a purely functional rider. To me the horse was just the most convenient form of conveyance for following my hounds. I always got there in the end.

I should tell you that I was never actually very fond of jumping fences. I did not enjoy that rather sick-making moment when you realized with awful inevitability that you were in the process of parting company with your other half who, probably weighing about 500 kgs, was about to roll on you. Some of the horses who partnered me over the years made quite a feature of that sort of thing; therefore I was never one to spurn an open gate when there was one at hand.

I would not want you to think that I do not appreciate a good horse. I have ridden so many moderate horses (and some downright bad horses) that I jolly well treasured the good ones when they came my way. I always had a Champagne taste in horses. Like good Champagne, good horses do not come cheaply and I always had a Sparkling Cider pocket. I was only able to buy a really good horse when it had had an 'if' about it: usually brake failure.

Being run away with on a horse is nobody's idea of fun; in fact, it is very frightening and can well end in tears — always supposing that you are conscious enough to cry at all (or ever again). These days, in the hunting field, it is often necessary for the followers to form an orderly queue for a wicket gate or a small post-and-rails put in for the hunt. A horse that has a violent objection to queueing is a dangerous liability. Unless these horses have a screw loose in the brain (I have had some of those too), the reason for their impatience is a very natural desire to be in front. Once in front with nothing before them but the hounds, they will often give you a dream of a ride; or a ride to dream about.

Five horses retain a special place in my affections: Red Knight, Tyrone, Trendsetter, Asian Gold and Rowantree.

Asian Gold had been round Aintree on two occasions. He had never been a huntsman's horse before he came to me. He thought the new life was absolutely spiffing. He celebrated the occasion of his first outing by bucking me off on the way to the first covert. When hounds found a fox and went chiming away, he celebrated further by bolting with me. I do not know how many of you will ever find yourselves bearing down on five strands of brand new barbed wire at thirty mph without the benefit of brakes but if you do, my advice is (a) to close your eyes, (b) to pray. Interested spectators (and there were not a few) tell me that the old horse took off twenty feet from the fence, cleared it by five feet, and landed twenty feet into the field on the other side. Galloping across this, I opened my eyes and promptly shut them again. A green lane led out of the field across which were two gates: between the two gates the farmer had obligingly confined some twenty bullocks. I do not know how many of you . . .; anyway, see (a) and (b) above. In the time I had him, the old boy never touched a fence (or a bullock) but always insisted on jumping in over-drive.

Just by the by: I do not think that you will find anything about closing the eyes and praying in any book on equitation; however, I have no hesitation in heartily recommending them to the Coarse Horseperson.

Rowantree was my last horse and probably the best. He

was a Rolls-Royce of a horse who purred with power. I only got him because his throttle cable kept jamming in the open position. In fact, all he wanted was to be in front, with nobody between him and the hounds he adored; then you could ride him with a cotton thread and one finger. He was a kind, gentle horse with great spirit and a heart like a bucket. He was trotting round the field one day when his great heart just stopped.

I would never get another like him and now I am not going to try.

Chapter Thirty-Five

BIRDS, BEASTS
AND GHOSTS

I DO NOT THINK that country people are as superstitious as they used to be; or at least they no longer admit to it. However, I know people who still touch their cap or make a salute on seeing a single magpie. In my youth I can remember people crossing themselves on seeing this handsome bird. A single magpie is supposed to be unlucky: the devil was supposed to disguise himself as a magpie when he was jaunting about the countryside. Mind you, multiple magpies have happier connotations:

'One for sorrow, two for mirth, three for a wedding, four for a birth, five for silver, six for gold, seven for a secret that's never been told.'

A lot of country people will not eat hare, which is passing strange when you consider what a delicious feed it is. They will be unable, or unwilling, to give you a reason for their distaste. I suspect that you will find that it goes back to the old belief that witches assumed the form of hares to travel about the country. There was an old lady who lived in Bilsdale in Yorkshire in the last century who was generally thought to have certain powers. The story goes that on one occasion the local harriers had a good hunt on a hare which was seen to disappear under the door of a barn. When the huntsman opened the door, there was no sign of the hare, but there was Old Granny Whatsit slumped on a mound of hay, puffing and blowing.

I am not knocking anyone's beliefs. I know that strange things happen and I know of people who have powers for which there is no apparent explanation. I once lived in a part of England where there were two local 'wise women'. One specialized in minor human ailments, warts and such like, whilst the other was absolute mustard on curing cattle, to the greater discomfort of the local veterinary practitioners.

People have sometimes asked me whether I believe in 'ghosts and all that old nonsense'. I do know that there are certain places where I would not go alone at night, even for an offer of much fine gold. I also lived in a haunted house for a time when I was a child and so the short answer is, 'Yes, I do.' Mind you, I never saw the ghost, but I often used to hear him at night. I reckon that it was a male ghost because he walked like an old man: shuffle, shuffle, shuffle, along the landing outside my room and down the stairs. I never saw anything because I was buried under the bed clothes, clutching my Daisy airgun and, anyway, I do not think that he ever tried to come into my room. The following morning, doors that had been shut would have been opened and lights that had been turned off would be on. That house had a nasty feel to it.

My parents lived for a long time in a house in Gloucestershire. That house was, and I hope is, a very happy place; nevertheless, a strange thing happened there.

I was alone in the house one winter's night, reading in front of the fire. Ginny, my terrier, was asleep at my feet. She suddenly got to her feet and stood rigid; her hackles were up and her teeth bared. She made no sound, and only her head moved as she watched something as it moved across the room from the door to the window, through which it presumably exited because she suddenly relaxed and curled up again at my feet as though nothing had happened. I neither saw, felt, nor heard anything. You may make of that what you will.

Foxes are always supposed to have some connection with the supernatural.

My favourite fox story concerns a certain noble earl who had his own pack of hounds in Nottinghamshire for thirty-five years. He had decreed that in the event of his death, hounds were to meet at a certain place on the day following the funeral, which they did. At this point, it is necessary to state that the old man had had a huge spreading grey beard. Hounds were taken to a patch of whins by the meet and up jumped a huge *grey* fox. A terrific hunt then took place in which the mounted followers were completely outpaced.

They eventually found the hounds.

They were sitting on the old earl's grave.

Chapter Thirty-Six

THE
TALE OF TWO
FRENCH BREAKFASTS

A s a Committed European, I think that it is time that I exploded the myth of the Continental Breakfast. The British hotel trade maintains it to be a frozen croissant, two pats of foil-wrapped butter and a cup of instant gunge distantly related to coffee.

This is the Tale of Two French Breakfasts.

Madame suggested that perhaps Monsieur-the-English would like a good breakfast before he went out the next morning? I said that I thought that that would be an absolutely ripping idea – in French, you understand.

Breakfast was served promptly at 0700. It consisted of two fried goose eggs (approximately equal to four hens' eggs), a plate of ham, a loaf of bread and a bottle of Premier Cru Volnay. Madame clucked with pleasure at my clean plate. She then produced home-made boar pâté, cheese, coffee and *eau de vie*. I must eat, she said, I would get nothing until at least 1030.

My friend Jeannot lives in a little house beside a lake in the heart of the forest. You may not be able to pinpoint the place from this description, but if I tell you that it is hard by the Bistro of the White Queen then I am sure that you will all know exactly where we are at.

Jeannot is a little brown nut of a man. He is a *garde du forêt*: a sort of bailiff-cum-ranger. He is also a dedicated follower of the local hunt and that was how I came to meet him. Before the day's hunting, there takes place a process which the French call *faire le bois* which I've described in chapter 20. It is the same process for deer as for wild boar: selected men walk different parts of the forest to find out exactly what is lieing where.

By arrangement I met Jeannot at the bar, Les Tilleuses, at 0700. He was already into his first coffee and firewater of the day. Cup and glass were placed before me as a matter of course. The café was full of workmen having their morning stiffener: a very apt description of the local *eau de vie*.

I shook hands all round. Another coffee and glass appeared in front of me. More men came and shook my hand. They do not get many Englishmen at Les Tilleuses. Four 'coffees-with' later we departed. All payment was indignantly refused.

A dozen men had gathered at Jeannot's house. There was more hand shaking, more coffee and more . . . yes, that is correct: how did you guess?

Deep in the forest there were more men; no coffee, but from each battered van anonymous bottles appeared.

Each group was issued with an aged hound on a lead to help the proceedings. We copped for César who is an old friend of Jeannot.

We walked. The French have been very sound about preserving their forests: oak, beech and birch still maintain. What a pleasure it was to walk on a springy bed of leaf mould with the early flowers beginning to show. Early infusions of *eau de vie* make one very philosophical.

Jeannot speaks no English and my French is basic but we communicated. Every so often he would stop and point. Deer had crossed the ride in the night. By the size of the prints and the length of the stride Jeannot could tell the age and sex of each deer. César's lack of interest indicated that none was close.

We walked for two hours and, Lo and Behold, we were back Chez Jeannot, and so were all the other lads.

We all pressed the flesh again. Then we all sat at a long table in a room with a huge open fire. I do not like Pernod, but by the second glass it was growing on me. A huge plate of charcuterie was put in front of me, with chunks of bread. I was quite sharp set by this time and thought that I had made an excellent breakfast.

Enter Madame Jeannot with massive dishes of chips. Plate-sized steaks materialized and were slapped on a grill over the fire.

The Pernod gave way to wine: lots of wine.

François waved a huge knife and said that it would do equally well for killing pigs or Englishmen.

I waved a bottle and said that if they did not behave I would sing to them.

This suggestion was received with enthusiasm.

So I did. Rapturous applause.

Another song. More wine.

Now it was time to fill the cracks with a morsel of cheese. Madame reappeared with coffee and, would you believe, *eau de vie*.

At the meet, I stood in line with the others and made my *rapport*; if I was swaying slightly I do not think that anyone noticed, and I was pleasantly surprised at how fluent my French had become.

The next time I go to France, I shall call on my friend Jeannot. He might invite me to breakfast again.

Chapter Thirty-Seven

THE
TANG AND TINGLE
OF AUTUMN

I AM ALWAYS GLAD to welcome autumn. The end of summer becomes stale, sticky and exhausted. The air feels sour, recycled and ghetto-blasted. The countryside is littered with discarded brown ale cans and crumpled crisp packets. Then, one early morning, you walk out of the door and there it is: an edge to the first breath; a sharpness, a tang, a tingle. It is the first sniff of autumn.

There are other signs too. The caravan site in the valley empties and is finally locked up until the spring. The roads become full of loads of straw, sometimes literally so if the loading of the trailer has not been everything it might. Across the valley, the brown stubbles change to chocolate colour as the ploughs crawl up and down. Sometimes the growl of heavy diesel engines can be heard into the small hours, as the work continues in the glare of tractor lights.

Autumn in the Cheviots can be a time of quite remarkable beauty, with September and October often being the best months of the year: brilliant sunny days with a crispy crunch in the air. Every breath seems to ream out the lungs.

On the hills the purple of the heather flowers fades, the bracken beds turn from dark green, through russet, to dark brown. I could wax lyrical about the colours of the autumnal hills; the browns, the greens, the purples; the cloud shadows racing over the great sweeping hillsides – but at the moment the hills are totally obscured by a lashing hail storm, so I will not. Autumn is not always kind and cooperative.

Autumn is a busy time for me both professionally and socially.

For an instance: there are the shows.

Local shows are alive and well and thriving in North-umberland. There is a show somewhere in the area every Saturday throughout the autumn. They happen in strict rota-tion so that everyone knows where they ought to be each weekend. The marquees (1 big, 1 smaller) trundle round from show to show, closely followed by the secretary's caravan, with the Mobile Ladies' Loo skipping along behind.

In the morning there is Showing of Sheep. The judge is some high-powered local sheep man and he has a steward which is very often me. I get chosen because it is rumoured that I am able to count up to three, for the placings, and I am deemed too fat to run off with the prize money that bulges my pockets.

Each pen of sheep is loosed into the ring. The judge looks them up and then he looks them down. He then gives each sheep a sharp double tap-tap with his stick and, as he does so, the owner catches it up and an orderly line forms from the top. The judge then does a minute inspection of eyes, teeth and fleece. He may rearrange the line a bit. He then gives the steward, who is smoking his pipe and dreaming quietly in the corner of the ring, a sharp prod with the stick and says, 'From the top, lad.'

In the big marquee, there is judging of cakes, produce, handicrafts, dressed sticks and (heaven help us) leeks. Show leeks need two men to carry them. They are grown under conditions of the utmost secrecy and top security, often guarded by fearsome dogs and equally fearsome owners armed with shotguns. Every year there are dark rumours of leeknap-ping, sabotage, and general vegetative mayhem. Leek-men are a dangerous species.

Outside the large marquee there will be other entertain-ments. Almost certainly there will be pony sports, a dog show, a greasy pole, wrestling, a tug of war, quoits, a sheep dog trial, a parade of the local foxhounds, a hound trail and sundry trade stands. The local Pipe Band's skirlings will per-vade the afternoon.

Meanwhile the show is gathering steam. You will no doubt have been bursting with impatience to know what happens in the second marquee: drinking is what happens. The inhabitants of the wild border hills live hard and lonely lives. On the occasions when they decide to have a day off, they put their hair in a figurative braid and set out to enjoy themselves in a determined manner. It is quite possible that their homes will not see them on the night of the show (the wife and bairns will look to the stock). Odd pieces of human detritus may well still be coming blearily back to normal during the next forty-eight hours. The drink tent will bulge at the seams by the end of the afternoon. It is a tribute to the well-balanced natures of most country people that there will be very little strife.

I think we might leave the show at this point. I mean, you do not want to sit up all night talking about collies and hounds and foxes, and singing and listening to really good fiddling, now do you?

The autumn is the time of harvest. As with corn, so with sheep: the autumn is the time of the sheep harvest and the culmination of a year's hard work. The lambs that are born in the spring are now ready to be converted into cash.

I usually manage to get a 'draw for the fat' in the early autumn before the goodness goes out of the grass. This means that some of the older lambs have made best use of the pasture and can now be deemed to be 'finished', or ready for the butcher. Most of my lambs go in the Store. That means that they are bought by farmers in the lusher south who will take them home and finish them on better keep.

The autumn is also the time of the great breeding sheep sales. The North of England is justly renowned for the excellence of its stock and stockmen. It is especially renowned for the Scottish Half Bred (Border Leicester X Cheviot) and the Mule (Blue Faced Leicester X Swaledale or Northumbrian Black Face). Buyers come from all over the country to buy these ewes and ewe lambs.

My tentative efforts at selling ewe lambs have not met with great success and I think that it is best left to the real experts and very good luck to them.

Some farmers love marts. For them, a sheep sale is not just business but a great social occasion as well. There they will meet friend and foe from miles around. There will be gossip and rumour and a glass or three. But the main talk will be of the sheep, the whole sheep and nothing but the sheep. All very jolly, I hear you say. In very small doses, say I.

Most marts are cheerless, windswept places and the Clerk of the Weather usually has his computer programmed for rain on mart day. Take several thousand sheep and hundreds of men; wet them thoroughly; then compress them into a small area; let them all perform the functions necessary to all animals during a long day; let them then all slosh about in it; what you have got is a sheep sale. It lacks romance. As you stand with the water dripping from your hat brim and the pipe turned upside down against the rain, you may feel a lack of intellectual stimulation.

Lorries grind up continously and disgorge yet more sheep.

'Ho! Ho! Mind your backs!' bellow the drovers as they try to get each lot of sheep to its numbered pen.

Farmers and shepherds lean on their sticks beside their pens, smoking and chatting and keeping a weather eye on the buyers who are creeping round the pens trying to look uninterested. There is a certain amount of static in the atmosphere. After all, six thousand lambs can turn over something like a quarter of a million quid and everybody wants a slice. Everybody wants to hear that the 'Yorkshiremen are up', or the big dealers from the Midlands. The rumour will whip round the pens like electricity.

It is the custom for the farmer to accompany his sheep into the ring to show his pride in his product, and to hold his stick in the air if the auctioneer looks like knocking them down too quickly. This lets buyer and auctioneer know that they have got to pull the finger and work a little harder. I actually hate going in the ring. I always feel a prize prat but, as my friends all tell me, that is nothing to what I look. The hammer falls. You take the sales chit from the clerk and watch the lambs being driven away. My feelings are always mixed. I have, after all, known those lambs since they were a twinkle in the tup's eye; now they will just be some numbers on a cheque – nice big ones, I hope.

So the autumn goes. The nights draw in. There will be crusts of ice on the puddles and troughs in the mornings. Great storms of wind and rain come howling out of the west and batter down the dying leaves. Then there are the still evenings that smell of frost and wood-smoke and are loud with the clatter of pheasants going to roost.

Winter is coming, and I like winter. I like the hard crisp mornings. I like the long evenings in front of the fire with pipe and book. Most of all I love the wild cry of hounds on the great, bare hills. But that, as they say, is another story.

I could wax lyrical about the colours of the autumnal hills

Chapter Thirty-Eight

A KEEN HAT
MAN

As WINTER APPROACHES, so does the time when every sensible person should be thinking about getting a hat. Did you know that you can lose thirty percent of your body heat through the top of your head? My theory is that a great deal of common sense and decency also goes up with the steam. Am I alone in noticing the decline in good manners and general behaviour since the wearing of hats went out of fashion? I suggest that a hat is a psychological as well as a physical lid. You may want it all to hang out but how unpleasant for those of us who have to watch it dangling, especially if it also has heavy catarrh.

I have always been a keen hat man. I have hats for every occasion and for every mood. The mood is important. I mean there are days when one is in a Flat Cap Mood. Then again, on another day, the hand might automatically reach for the battered furry trilby-type hat hanging on one of the hooks. I suppose that you are going to ask me what the difference might be between a Flat Cap Mood and a Trilby Mood. People who ask questions like that are never likely to understand the answers. A true Hat Person would instinctively understand.

I was brought up with hats.

I have somewhere a picture of myself, aged single figures, peering out from between a huge sou'-wester and a suit of oil skins. My father was something of a blue-nosed sailor and a great part of my formative years was spent laying out my kit off various parts of the Cornish coast.

As a young man I spent four grinding years at a Dickensian office in the City. The only thing that cheered me up was the purchase of my first bowler hat. I very much regret the decline of that most useful piece of headgear. It was originally designed by Coke of Holkham to protect the bonces of his gamekeepers from the cudgels of the roughs, and were therefore good hard hats. The modern generation are poor, flimsy, whimpering things by comparison. It is still a very well designed hat for the wet and is also excellent for ratting after dinner, when one goes with the terriers and a stick and a torch into the old pig house where the rats swarm along the beams. The bowler hat prevents a rat down the neck. In case you are thinking of having a go at this interesting business, I also recommend wellington boots. A rat up the trouser leg is a deplorable situation both for you and the rat. Apart from ratting, nowadays my bowler hat only goes to Peterborough Hound Show and to funerals. Bowler hats are seldom seen in London anymore: passing sad.

I have never been a great felt hat man. I sometimes used to wear a felt hat to go to London, or on the odd occasion when I used to go racing. Then someone used my felt hat to be sick into and I have never felt the same about that person, or the hat, since. The wide brimmed hat is not actually very practical because, although it does keep the rain off the back of the neck, it also tends to blow off in a wind; unless, of course, you tie a bit of baler string over the crown and under the chin.

Yes, I am really more of a Flat Cap person.

The one drawback to the flat cap is that it does not keep the neck dry.The feeling of water trickling down the back of the neck is one of the most dispiriting that I know. It is only capped (if you will excuse the expression) by the steady seepage of water into the base area. The latter problem can be avoided by wearing waterproof trousers. The wet-neck problem can be solved by the good old-fashioned deerstalker hat.

Many of you will be aware of the deerstalker as the hat worn by Sherlock Holmes: peaked fore and aft and with ear flaps. You may have thought of them as quaint Victorian relics. In fact, they are alive and well and have remained living quietly in the remoter parts of the realm. They are extremely practical. The forepeak keeps the sun out of the eyes, whilst the bit that sticks out aft (which I suppose cannot be a peak) deflects the rainwater. The flaps keep the ears warm and stop the whole thing taking off in a gale. I have never been very keen on those little ribbons to tie under the chin (try doing it with chilled-to-the-bone fingers) so I replace those with Velcro straps.

Deerstalkers are coming back into fashion amongst the Chattering Classes. I know this because I went into the gents in a famous London store the other day. The only other occupant was wearing white shoes, a pinstripe suit, yellow shirt and a pink-and-grey checked deerstalker hat.

Chapter Thirty-Nine

THE 'NEW' FORESTRY COMMISSION

I HAVE ALWAYS GOT on well with the Forestry Commission at the personal level, but I have not always been an unreserved admirer of their handiwork.

Until recently, the received wisdom of the Commission seemed to have been to plant as many trees as were viable (and some that were not) in the space available. It was thought that the most efficient way to do this was to put in neat geometrically-shaped plantations of trees of the same age. The most efficient tree available was the Sitka spruce. The result has been what many people have come to regard as an alien imposition covering some of the more beautiful parts of our countryside. I think it is fair to say that many old Forestry Commission hands developed a somewhat geometric attitude themselves. On occasion, outsiders tended to bump up against the sharp edges.

To be fair to the foresters of the past, they were only following the remit that they were given in 1919, which was to make Britain self-sufficient in timber needs. They may not have been very imaginative to the needs of landscape and conversation, but then these were not great point of pressure at that time.

Today the Forestry Commission has a different outlook.

Martin Gale is the Forest Commission District Manager at Rothbury. He is a good example of the new thinking in the Commission: a passionate and articulate Man of Trees. Recently, he was kind enough to take me with him on his rounds.

We started at the plantation on Howe Moor which was the first planting in the Rothbury Forest in 1921. As this is a relatively sheltered spot, it was planted with Douglas fir. These magnificent trees are just coming to maturity: the first block (or 'felling coupe') has already been felled and replanted. I was intrigued by the rather straggling clump of Scots pine that had been left standing in the felled area, and was delighted to learn that they have been left to feed the red squirrels who still thrive in this area. It is now Commission policy to include some suitable conservation measure into each replanted area.

The Commission recently purchased 1000 acres of heather hill and this was our next stop.

A personal thought at this point. I am a sheep farmer. It is my strongly-held opinion that land belonging to good sheep farms should not be planted. They should be kept for sheep and the families who live by them. However, there are areas of the hills which are so hard and sour that they are better under trees. This particular hill has not been farmed with any great enthusiasm.

Martin finds the area an exciting prospect because it gives the Commission a chance to incorporate all the new thinking on forest planning. The aim is to avoid the huge regimented blocks of the past. In the future, forest planting will be required to complement the landscape. The boundaries of the different blocks will follow natural features such as watercourses and existing tracks. There will be ten-year age differences between each 'felling coupe' to avoid dreary uniformity. Twenty percent of the area will be planned as open space (leaving watercourses, scenic slopes and rock faces unplanted) although there will be strategically placed broadleaved copses in the open spaces. To help with this planning, the Commission makes use of aerial and long-distance ground survey. The Rothbury District has also recently taken on a full time Landscape Architect: a very positive step.

The commercial aims of the planting cannot be ignored but with some imagination commercial woodland can not only look good but can be made to operate as a wildlife habitat. That is the current thinking.

Yardhope is the 'Conservation Jewel of Rothbury Forest'. It

is based on an ancient oak wood in a steep and secret valley. There are records of these oaks being worked in 1327. At one time there would have been many of these old scrub oak woods in the river valleys; Yardhope is one of the few to survive and the Forestry Commission intends to see that it continues to do so. The old trees are not regenerating in a very satisfactory way and the seedlings are ravaged by a particular species of oak leaf-eating caterpillars. A 150-year plan of selective felling and replanting with seedlings reared in nurseries has begun. This should ensure that Yardhope will survive and flourish in the future.

I found my day interesting and thought provoking. I was forced to rethink some of my prejudices, because the Forestry Commission had beaten me to it and rethought some of theirs.

It seems obvious that with the changes that are taking place in farming we are going to see more trees planted on the low ground as well as on the hills. There will be more scope for broadleaved species on the better ground, but Sitka will always be the 'bread and butter' tree on the harsher land. I shall never grow to love it. I should like to see oak, ash and rowan but, sadly, they are not commercial and the Forestry Commission has to turn its shilling like all the rest of us.

The last word to Martin Gale: 'Asking us to grow oaks commercially on the hills is like asking a Northumbrian farmer to grow pineapples.'

Chapter Forty

HACKING HOME

CHAMBERS DICTIONARY HAS several different definitions for 'hack'. The ones that concern me are: (n) a person overworked on hire: a literary or journalistic drudge: and (v.i.) to journey on horseback.

Until fairly recent times, if you wanted to go hunting, you rode your horse to the place of meeting, hunted and then rode home afterwards; often in the dark. You 'hacked'.

There was little alternative. Motorized horse transport did not become general until the sixties. I had no transport until 1964. By the same token, there was little traffic on rural roads and what there was tended to be slow and cautious.

Some hunts were well served by the old railway system. At one time you could cause a railway horse box to be tacked on to most passenger trains and to have it dropped off at some convenient station. There were even special hunt trains with hound van, horses boxes and carriages. Certain hunts had their own rolling-stock and I remember an old man telling me that you could hire an engine and crew for the day for the princely sum of 3 guineas.

Times have changed.

The railways will no longer transport any animals larger than a dog except (grudgingly and in acute discomfort) the human animal. Many roads are now unsafe for horses in daylight; none is safe in the dark, even in the country. Unless they can see opposing headlights, most rural drivers consider the road to be all their very own. Nowadays hounds and horses are boxed even short distances.

There are people who wax nostalgic about the joys of hacking home in the frosty winter sunset with the blackbirds chinking in the hedges. My response to this is 'horsefeathers'.

I, too, have memories of hacking home: collecting hounds in the burgeoning dark, wet through and chilled to the bone, horse tired and missing a shoe, the first tentacles of incipient influenza groping the system, perhaps a four-, or five-hour journey in front of you: hounds and horses to 'do up' before you get near the fire; and yes, what fun, it is starting to snow.

Progress is a dry overcoat, a warm lorry cab, and a thermos of hot tea at the end of the day: that is the sort of progress that I heartily approve of.

Mind you the old days did produce some interesting moments.

A certain man went hunting with a pack of hounds adjacent to his own. It was a day of teeming rain. They had a great hunt and finished up in the dusk many miles on the other side of the country.

In the course of the day, the Visitor had conversed with a Native of the Country. Foxhunters are hospitable folk and the Native suggested that the Visitor should return with him to his adjacent home where bed, board and dry clothing would be available for man and horse.

On arrival at the Native's house, the Visitor was taken up to the Native's dressing-room where dry clothes were laid out for him, the Native and the Visitor being of very similar build.

The Native's Lady had been absent when the hunters arrived back. On her own return, loving spouse that she was, she went at once in search of her mate.

The Visitor had gladly removed his sodden nether garments and was struggling to get his wet, clinging shirt over his head.

He heard the door open.

A returned wife entering her husband's dressing-room and seeing there a man naked except for a shirt over his head is likely to make certain assumptions; especially if what she sees does not differ greatly from what she is accustomed to seeing. A humorous lady may then feel that a little conjugal jape is in order.

The Visitor, still struggling with his shirt, found gentle

advantage being taken of his person and heard a soft voice saying: 'Tinkle, tinkle: time for tea,' followed by peals of silvery laughter.

The silvery laughter continued all the way down the stairs and into the drawing-room where the lady found her full-clad husband leaning on the mantelpiece.

Chapter Forty-One

THE WINTER
IN THE BORDERS

I LIKE WINTER. In this part of the world it tends to be clean and hard. Our prevailing wind is westerly. It whips up the Irish Sea and whoops across 100 miles of bracken and heather until it comes battering on my windows. I like the west wind. It may be a bit boisterous on occasion but, by and large, it is good natured.

I am not so keen on winter when the wind gets into the east and especially the south-east: this is a 'bad airt' (direction). All our really bad weather comes on the south-east wind. It is a bad, mean, totalitarian wind. It brings in the grey weeping clouds off the North Sea and the damp cold seeps into the bones and the dank dreariness saps the soul. All the bad snows come out of the south-east: the thick belt of Sitka spruce that protects my steading from the east, keeps the worst of the weather off the buildings, but my road will be blocked at the end of the wood and the only way out will be to plough out. This is when we hope for the quick return of the west wind.

Winter is a quiet time on the farm. The hectic round of sheep sales and markets is done. I always heave a sigh of relief when the last batch of lambs has been sold and the seemingly endless round of dosing, jagging (injecting) and ovine pedicure quietens down.

Through November and December the tups (rams) are out with the ewes (ask Mummy if you do not know why). Apart from changing the tups about from one lot of ewes to another (you had better have a word with Daddy this time), the flock is best left alone to let Mother Nature work her little miracle. But they do need feeding. I give my ewes a ration of concentrates right through the tupping time. (Please do not bother to write to me and tell me how wrong I am. I know that your father and grandfather never fed their ewes and I am sure that you do not either, but I do. And yes, the farm did make a (small) profit last year.)

I like feeding sheep and I like the early mornings, so I do the concentrate round before breakfast.

Mind you, I do not like it if it is raining. Nothing is much pleasure in the rain. But we live in a low rainfall area, 28 inches p.a., I think. I would not like to live in Borrowdale or wherever it is that the annual rainfall is 130 inches: I should get mildew.

The first part of the morning routine is to stand in the door, have a good scratch and see what sort of day it is. The next thing is to let the collies out. We exchange matutinal felicitations and muddy pawmarks. We go together to fetch the ATV. This is a four-wheeled motorbicycle with a carrying platform fore and aft. On each platform I place a bag of concentrates.

The ewes will have been listening for the sound of the engine and there will be chorus of complaint at the appalling slackness of the service ('One simply cannot get good staff these days, dear'). They are waiting in an impatient bunch as I chug into the field.

Cobs are what I use. They are knobs about the size of a lump of smokeless fuel. You just open the bag and run out a long trail along the ground: simple? It is not quite so simple. A Mule ewe weighs approximately 150 lbs. A Mule ewe is the greediest thing on this earth; a Mule ewe would trample its own mother, grandmother and/or child to get to the grub first. There are 120 Mule ewes in each bunch. At the first rustle of a bag, they go spare. To lie on your back on the muddy ground being comprehensively stabbled by 480 sharp little feet is not a good way to start the day.

The dogs deal with the matter. Whilst I am opening the bag, they keep the ewes back in a corner. I can then drop out a nice neat line of cobs without interference.

'That'll do.' The dogs stand back and the stampede is under-way.

Then it is back to breakfast. As one crosses the yard, blowing on the frozen fingers, the nose curls itself around the first hint of cooking bacon. There may be better smells on a frosty morning, but I do not know what they are.

With the farm work on a care and maintenance base, there is time for other things in the backwoodsman's life. For me, and for many thousands of other people, the winter means foxhunting. For many years it was my whole life. Now it is no more than a Grand Passion. I gave up riding horses when I gave up being directly involved with the hounds, but I still hunt every day that my other work allows.

Rupert takes me hunting. Rupert is my ATV. Why Rupert? Robert (age nine) is my neighbour's son. He kept asking me what my bike was called, so, in desperation, I called it Rupert. Rupert has ten forward gears (+ reverse), four-wheel drive, a 350-cc engine and low ground pressure tyres. He carries me, Jess the terrier, my thermos and sandwiches, a spade for digging me out, and my stick in case I want to walk.

The following of our little hunt consists almost entirely of farmers, shepherds and farmworkers who live and work in the border hills. They look to the hunt for their sport and also as a practical means of keeping the fox population within reason-able bounds come lambing time.

The meet is just a piece of flat ground up the valley where there is room to park the lorries and trailers. The great bare hillsides sweep up on either side, green and brown, with grey clitters of rock cascading down them. There are, perhaps, forty horses, twenty cars and a dozen shepherds on their bikes.

Little time is wasted at the meet, for the days are short at this time of year.

The huntsman sets away up a steep sheep trod and hounds are soon fanned out across the bare hill, their white coats standing out against the dark ground. Most of us stay on the valley road where there is the best view at this point.

Some hounds have come together in a line and are working busily, their sterns lashing. They are touching the drag where a fox has been through that morning. There is a faint whimper which becomes a full chorus as more hounds join the line.

'There he is!' Pointing fingers, swivelling binoculars. There he is indeed: a dark red form slipping effortlessly across the jumbled rock face where he had lain up after his night's foraging. We watch him out over the top and watch the hounds as they come streaming on the line, their fierce wild cry and the thrilling cheer of the huntsman echoing in the valley.

All is action now. The line of cars surges up the road. The horses face the steep climb out over the hill.

It is decision time. I have to choose left or right to get to a place where I can cross the river and climb the hill. Hounds are over the top and out of sight: if I choose wrong, I may not see them again for some time.

Up up, straight up, standing on the foot rests to keep my weight thrown forward; Jess in the bag across my back with just her head sticking out, whining in excitement.

At the top of the hill the wind strikes savagely into the face – but what a view: a huge bowl of ground with the hills rolling in on all sides. The hounds are sweeping along the far edge of the bowl like a flock of gulls; two red coats going well on the flank and the mounted tail coming on behind. The cry comes very faintly on the gale.

Hounds are swinging right-handed all the time. A fox seldom runs dead straight: he usually has an angle. Now, if I am right, I am in quite a good place and if I just keep quiet and keep my eyes open, I might ... Yes, by golly, there he is! A big, red fox moving easily and unhurriedly across the rough ground. He is coming right to me. I ease myself down behind the bike and clamp my hand over Jess's muzzle. I feel her go rigid when she sees the fox. He comes up the hill in an steady lope, sees the bike, jinks slightly and puts on a spurt as he disappears over the hill.

I get to my feet and loose Jess's muzzle whereupon she lets fly with a most appalling stream of invective.

The deep cry is swelling now as hounds come swinging up the hill towards me and I feel that old familiar prickle at the back of the neck. As they drive past me, I cannot resist cheering them on for old times' sake.

'Four minutes in front,' I shout to the huntsman as he thunders past, his face streaked with mud and black bog mould and a grin from ear to ear: happy man. And if I feel a little twinge of regret for great times past as I stuff Jess back in her bag and climb onto the bike that is no one's business but mine own.

Looking at the day

Chapter Forty-Two

THE REALITY
OF RURAL LIFE

D O YOU DREAM OF living in the country? Many people tell me how they yearn for the Rustic Idyll and how Great-Grandfather Yandle (on Mother's side of the family) used to farm in Devon. It does seem to be an established fact that nearly all agricultural forebears came from Devon. I can only suppose that a diet of cider, pasties and unlimited clotted cream must have worked wonders for the libido of the elders. However, I do beg leave to wonder whether all these nice people would really like genuine rusticity.

Many people suffer from the 'Thatched Cottage Syndrome'. They see themselves living in a little thatched cottage with roses round the door and hollyhocks in the front garden. The cottage is situated in a picture postcard village on which there is perpetual sunshine. It is a 'closely knit community' where everybody smiles and bakes cakes all the time.

It is a lovely dream and everyone should have a dream. The secret, however, is to think twice before putting dreams to the test of reality.

Rural life can be very real.

The first thing that the Newcomers did was to tidy up the garden at Thatched Cottage. Old Tom Soady had let it go a bit, even if there was an unrivalled collection of rusty buckets and nettles. The Newcomers pulled out the old fence and made a lovely open-plan garden right across the front, doing away with the old track up the side of the house which did not seem to serve any useful purpose.

Everybody admired the garden.

Then the Septic Tank stirred its muscles. The Newcomers had never actually had a septic tank in the family before. They poured bleach and detergent down the drain as had been their wont in Woking. The Septic Tank stirred in its sleep and produced a *smell*.

The 'Cundy Keeker' was summoned to pump it out. This meant his backing his tanker up the side of the cottage — where that pointless old track had been, and across all those lovely new flower beds. The Locals all said that they knew that would happen. At least, the Locals knew where the tank was. There was the sad case of the mechanical digger sent in to locate a slumbering tank. It found it all right. It drove over it. The pit collapsed and ... Well, I think we will leave it there: the driver did.

As things turned out, there was little point in worrying about the damage to the flower beds. Three days later Jan Brimblecome (he comes from Devon, too) was bringing two hundred wild and hairy suckler cows (plus calves) through the village. The cow (plus calves) rejoiced exceeding in the Newcomers' open-plan garden.

The Newcomers had a nice new fence made. The following week Tommy Varco backed his tractor and trailer through it; having always been used to turning in Tom Soady's old track, he quite forgot it was no longer there.

The Newcomers had looked forward to 'taking part in the community' and making a positive contribution to local life. They privately felt that the community would benefit from a little urban zest.

Mr Newcomer was most gratified to find himself very quickly installed as Hon Sec of the local Horticultural Society. What he could not have known was that the Horticultural Society was the cock pit in which was fought out a feud of ancient and unimaginable bitterness between two of the village clans. He would stagger home from the meetings psychologically bloody and begrimed from the battle in which he figured as the Civilian Casualty.

The Newcomers were committed and caring people. They had been accustomed to sharing and discussing their concerns with others of a like mind when they lived in the town.

Mr Newcomer found the Drovers' Arms lacklustre on Nuclear Disarmament but hot and strong on Capital Punishment, Racial Purity and Immigration, especially when it came to the inhabitants of Nether Muxworthy. It seemed that the inhabitants of Nether Muxworthy were of inferior stock, whose curious habits precluded them from mixing in decent society (or Upper Muxworthy).

Mr Newcomer found the staples of conversation — sheep, corn, sheep, foxes, pheasants, sheep and the van that was parked outside Rose Cottage every night — rather limiting.

It also started raining the day the Newcomers moved in and (very probably) has not stopped since. The thatch leaked promiscuously and they had to have a line of buckets in their bedroom to catch the drips. The thatcher had been last heard of in Torremolinos.

The Septic Tank revolted again.

A lady from the village 'obliges' Mrs Newcomer in the house. The half of the village that is not related to the obliging lady now refuses to speak to the Newcomers.

I do not know whether the Newcomers will survive their dream-come-true, or not. Sometimes I think I see a faraway look in their eyes. It may just be my imagination but I think I see in that look an image of a nice little flat in Brighton, nice and near the shops and not too far from the Front.

May all your dreams come true.

Chapter Forty-Three

THE AMERICAN HUNTING ODYSSEY

Foxhunting in the USA is different.

I knew it was going to be different when we drove to the first meet. The lovely blonde lady was telling me about the day they had had at the Remainder Sale at the Friendly Neighborhood Whorehouse in her Old Home Town.

In England lovely blonde hunting ladies do not speak to me at all, not even about the WI jumble sale.

There has been foxhunting in America from the time of the first settlements. Not only did the pioneers bring their hounds with them, but (finding the native grey fox a rather disappointing quarry) they also imported the red fox from Europe. Today both the red and the grey fox are hunted. The bob cat is also hunted in certain parts and also coyote (pronounced kiyote) where applicable.

Virginia is generally regarded as the birthplace of American hunting. The traditional form of American hunting was a lot of people keeping perhaps one or two hounds and joining together for a hunt, sometimes by day, and sometimes by night. This tradition still maintains throughout the eastern states and more of it anon.

In the last century many hunts established themselves on a more formal pattern, very often forming Hunt Clubs and conducting their sport on anglicized lines. There are currently about 130 'recognized' packs of foxhounds in the USA.

At a quick glance, formal American hunting might look the same as the English version and, indeed, many Americans fervently believe that it is.

It is a bit like an old house that has come under new (and wealthier) ownership. The new owners have carefully preserved the outer shell but, inside, the house has been rebuilt, rewired and replumbed to suit their notions of comfort; and why not? I can think of many Britons who would think that the American style was absolutely the buttered waffle. Indeed, I can think of certain packs in England who have pretty well adopted the American style, even though they would probably hotly deny it. I know that it would drive me to paroxysms of frustration (it did), but then I am an old hard case foxhunter and probably an anachronism.

The next thing to say is that nowhere will you find more charming, courteous or hospitable people than you will find in the southern states of America.

First stop Lexington, Kentucky.

Kentucky is probably more famous for bloodstock than foxhunting, but hunting there is. My visit coincided with a visit to Kentucky by the great Mr Hardaway. There will be more, much more, about this remarkable man. For the moment, it is sufficient to say that he had made the eleven-hour journey from Georgia with fifteen horses and thirty couple of hounds for six solid days' hunting with the local hunts.

The first day's hunting was to be with the Woodford hounds.

The Woodford hounds are a fairly new pack who live, would you believe, in Woodford County. Theirs is a country of rolling pastureland with deep wooded creeks. They have Walker hounds. I am informed that there are about fourteen different types of American hound: Bywaters, Trigs, July, Brunswick, Penn Mardyel ... The Walkers have renowned stamina but are about as biddable as a disused steam boiler.

At the meet, there was a cameraman from the *Woodford Argus*. I told him that I was from the London *Telegraph*. He asked after several London acquaintances and expressed surprise that I did not know the K.T. Drugstore on Main Street. Well, of course, you will all have twigged that he thought I was from London, Kentucky (which lies between Manchester and Somerset) where they talk funny anyway.

It was a day of stunning autumn beauty. The sun was hot, the crickets were stridulating, the buzzards were soaring and the crows were making the extraordinary noise that American crows make. Somewhere deep in the creek the combined Woodford and Midland hounds were speaking to the drag of a fox. It was all rather pleasing, and I would happily have sat on my hill top, in the sun, listening. But there was the problem of Mary Anna's Appetite.

Mary Anna is small, very beautiful, and eats like a shark. There was nothing for it but for our little party to embus and head for the only store in miles. As I have explained, I do not ride anymore and having had a quick look at American hunt jumps I was glad that I did not. Bird, who had volunteered to drive us about, had a broken collar bone as a result of a hunt jump. She managed to drive very fast, steering and changing gear with one hand: most interesting. After we had vastly ensandwiched Mary Anna, we found the hounds again and just missed our first American fox who was being pursued with tremendous enthusiasm in ever-decreasing circles.

The centre of these proceedings was a farmhouse. There was a man on the roof nailing things over holes. I assume that he was the landed proprietor, but he seemed strangely unmoved by the stirring events taking place around his farm. At last he paused in his hammering and, leaning down to me (as an obviously authoritative figure) said: 'Mistuh, what y'all doin' with all those dawgs?'

'Foxhunting,' I said.

'Holy shit!' he said and he went back to his hammering.

By now it was getting dimpsey and it was decided that hunting should cease. It was Party Time.

An *obiter dictum*: The Americans do not favour very long days. They seem either to meet at nine and stop about midday, when there may be a hunt breakfast; or they meet at one and stop at about four, when it is nicely time for a party — and jolly well they do you, too.

Charley and Pam Walker gave the party after hunting in their splendid old colonial house. I started on some in-depth research, which continued throughout the visit, into the relative therapeutic qualities of Straight and Sour Mash Bourbon

Whisky. A kind man shook his head as he poured me another generous stiffener. He told me that his wife stayed as sweet as honey so long as she drank martinis, but she was 'mean clean through her bones on one drink of Scotch.'

The next day we all drove about seventy miles to the Long Run Hunt, near Louisville.

The Long Run is being squeezed by development and roads. Their huntable country only measures five miles by four and they somehow contrive to hunt it two days a week. I had a jolly day being driven about in great state by 'C.J.', a retired General Officer who had a very well-stocked vehicle which enabled me to continue my researches. I cannot in all honesty report on the hunting because they only found one fox and it went into a hole within quarter of a mile.

The dinner was given by Mr and Mrs Ed Bonnie and was what in Yorkshire they would call 'a Grand Feed'.

I eventually persuaded a lovely Georgian Lady Doctor to feel my pulse. She said: 'Honey, the amount of liquor y'all consoom, you shouldn't rightly have a pulse.'

The Long Run people are charming people and I am full of admiration for the way they overcome the difficulties of their country.

The next day was the turn of the Iroquois. This hunt takes its name from the racehorse not the Indian tribe who lived up north anyway; the local Indians were Cherokee and Shoshone and Daniel Boone used to live just down the road. Kentucky is Cherokee for 'the dark and bloody ground' and do not say that you never get any culture from your correspondent.

We met at Caveland, the home of Dr and Mrs Holloway who had been a tremendous help in organising my trip. This part of Kentucky is truly beautiful and reminded me of parts of the Cotswolds. It was a glorious day with the temperature up in the 70s.

Mr Hardaway was hunting his hounds that day. There was a large and well turned out field that included my first sighting of the elusive American Top Hat. There was also a lady in a pony and trap which had been specially adapted to take her and her wheelchair. I thought that this showed a special sort of form.

There is no doubting the courage of American Equitators. Broken limbs are taken as a matter of course and seem much more prevalent than in Britain. I suspect that there are three reasons for this: (1) the ground is much harder; (2) they build themselves horrible obstacles; (3) many falls result from galloping into the ground hog holes that bespatter every field: a fall on the flat is always nasty. Another result of this mayhem is that there are a great number of hunting orthopaedic surgeons.

A fox had been seen crossing one of the home paddocks shortly before the meet so we all got rather excited and whizzed about trying to find him, but to no avail – he had popped into a hole.

Hounds found two other foxes during the day which also went to ground, so once again I cannot really comment on the hunting. Mr Hardaway, ever the master of the pithy one-liner, passed on his thoughts to me at the end of the day. I totally agreed with what he said, but I do not think that any of you are quite ready for that sort of thing.

Kentucky is a lovely place with lovely people and lots of laughs, but it was time to go to Virginia.

Virginia is difficult to write about. The ladies and gentlemen of Virginia take their pre-eminence in American hunting for granted and very seriously. The last English journalist who wrote about them failed to take them seriously and caused great offence. I have absolutely no desire to give offence.

Virginia is very beautiful: great rolling fields of old grass, fenced with timber or stone walls: nice little coverts, the whole thing manicured and kept for hunting with no expense spared. There are very few bits of hunting country left in England to compare with the best of Virginia.

The followers are beautifully turned out and mounted on the best (which = $10,000-20,000).

Everything should be set fair for the best foxhunting.

And yet ... and yet I decided that it was stupid to go to America with preconceived ideas and then be disappointed. It was stupid to apply my puritan zeal for the chase and the massive orthodoxy of my English ideas to the American situation. The Americans have taken formal foxhunting and adapted it to *their* country and *their* way of life and that is entirely *their* affair.

We stayed with Albert and Jackie Poe. Albert is huntsman of the Middleburg. His brother Melvin has been huntsman of the Orange County for nearly forty years. The Brothers Poe are the most famous professional huntsmen in America and deserve their fame.

We hunted with the Old Dominion and the Piedmont; ably driven by Peggy (Mrs Melvin Poe) or Jackie (with her arm in a sling). But the best day in Virginia was when we managed to hunt with both Poe brothers in one morning.

The Middleburg hounds caught a fox right in front of us. I got fearfully excited and leaped up and down, as is my wont. I have to say that most of those present, including the hounds, seemed rather embarrassed by this break with American tradition.

By the time we got to the Orange County, the morning was well on and the scent was fading and it was time for the Hunt Breakfast — but not before Melvin had fortified us with some Fox Grape Wine. Strange as it may seem, this is wine made from the Fox grape. It has remarkable diuretic properties; amongst other things.

In case you are thinking of 'breakfast' in terms of a bacon butty and a mug of tea, I have to say that it is not like that. At your American Hunt Breakfast, the browsing and sluicing is of the very best. People come from far and wide to join in the frolic. Those who have been hunting wear their hunting clothes. Some of those who have not been hunting wear their hunting clothes. The remainder of those who have not been hunting come dressed in their very, very best. My wife and I were not exactly fashion plates, but once again I was struck by the efforts Americans make to make strangers feel welcome. I am afraid that we do not do so well by them.

I felt very sorry for one lady who quizzed me about hunt breakfasts in England. She was reluctant to believe me when I said that we did not have them. Poor lamb, she had just purchased at great expense a 'Genuine English Hunt Breakfast Table'.

To Georgia.

Always leave the best until last.

The best in America is Benjamin H. Hardaway III. He will not be in the least bit embarrassed by this statement because he will heartily endorse it and, in his own words, 'feed on it like a tiger'.

Ben is a big man in every way. Again in his own words, he is 'big enough, rich enough, and mean enough to have what I want'. What he wants is foxhunting: lots and lots of foxhunting. He collected his first hounds when he was twelve years old. At the age of sixty-nine he still hunts his own hounds four days a week.

At the time of my visit, there were 238 hounds in the kennel and something like thirty horses in the stable. All the hunt staff have college degrees. Hardaway stamps about roaring and 'working their butts off' and they think that he is the best thing since Mother's cooking. Subscribers to the Midland Hunt only pay $25.00 because that is 'all the amount of say they get'. They are also a devoted band.

There are three different hunting countries: one around the Hardaway home at Midland, Georgia, and two separate territories in Alabama.

The Midland hounds catch more foxes per season than any other pack in America. I suspect that the Midland tally would surpass the combined total of all the other packs. They also hunt bobcat and coyote.

My first day with the Midland was at Cedar Heights in Alabama. This is a derelict cotton plantation in a rolling country of pines and scrub. With the temperature in the 70s, my expectation were not great.

I was wrong.

The Midland hounds are American July hounds with a judicious mixture of English Fell and West Country Harrier blood. Their cry is one of the best that I have ever heard; they do not lack speed and drive either. To demonstrate these qualities, they found a fox and were quickly out of our hearing despite the spirited efforts of Lyn, our driver, to keep in touch along the slithery back country dirt roads.

Hounds put this fox to ground after a flying thirty minutes. They then found another and disappeared again, this time leaving everyone wrongfooted.

All the Midland hunt staff carry portable radios. The hound van has a telescopic mast which covers a ten-mile radius. The radios now came into play and we eventually heard that Jesse, the Kennel Huntsman, had found the hounds, 'covered in varmint blood'.

It was now 2 pm and very hot so we stopped and Mrs Frank Carroll, wife of the Joint Master, produced great boxes of luncheon.

That night we went night hunting.

The hunting at night of fox and racoon is a strong and thriving American tradition. It is quite simple. Various men will bring their hounds in their pick-up trucks to a pre-arranged spot, loose them into the darkness, then sit around sipping, telling each other lies about their hounds, and listening to the cry until day break when the hounds are (hopefully) collected up and everyone goes home.

The preacher and his friends had brought their hounds to Ed's house. They were already hunting in the dark when we arrived. We went in and had dinner: southern fried beef, southern fried venison, collard greens, crowder peas, corn pudding: down home cooking.

It is my considered opinion that there are many worse ways of spending a nice warm evening than sitting in a rocking chair on a verandah with a bottle of Bourbon whisky to hand, whilst the cry of hounds ebbs and swells in the darkness all around. I suppose that we left about midnight. Hounds were still running strongly in the night.

The Grand Finale. The last day of the hunting Odyssey was at Fitzpatrick. This is Hardaway's other country in Alabama. He maintains a house there, which is inevitably known as 'Fox-patrick'.

This is lovely wild country of rolling savannahs interspersed with creeks and swamps. It is also deep back country where large silent men drive pick-up trucks with rifles and shot guns behind the seat. Every road sign is riddled with bullet holes. It is a country where a lone visitor might do well to tread delicately.

We all went down the night before and several other hunters gathered at the house to dine and sleep and follow that good American custom that is referred to as 'just knocking the dust off one'.

The meet was at the Log Run, which is not anywhere.

Hugh Bernard, a night hunter of great experience, had been summoned to drive the Scribe who was also given a radio. Within a short time, hounds were speaking, then the cry swelled. It was tremendous: my back hairs were prickling.

Radio Traffic: 'You hear that, Willypoo?'

'I hear it, Hardaway.'

'Hotdammit! Ain't they singing the blues.'

'It's a coyote! It's a coyote!' This from Jesse.

'Hotdammit! They really burning his ass!'

And indeed they were, to the extent that the coyote straightened out and headed for Texas. There was some hard galloping for the mounted followers and some furious driving by Hugh along glutinous dirt tracks. I felt that we ought to have had 'Foggy Mountain Breakdown' on the soundtrack. Instead, there was a considerable amount of excited 'Radio Hardaway', the burthen of which was that if he caught the coyote he was going to ram it head first up Willypoo's base area. You may be relieved to hear that this unusual physical challenge never bore the test.

After a gruelling two hours, the temperature (pushing 80) ground things to a halt. Hounds had made an eight-mile point and must have covered at least twice that distance.

'Hardaway,' I said, as we shook hands on parting and in my new found southern accent, 'Hardaway, y'all are the *king*,' and I meant it.

He grinned his wicked grin: 'Willypoo, y'all better believe it,' and he meant it too.

Chapter Forty-Four

CHRISTMAS MISANTHROPY

SOMEWHERE IN MY bound copies of *Punch* magazine there is a cartoon entitled the 'Bachelor's Christmas Dinner'. It shows a man sitting alone at a table chomping away with what is meant to be a mournful expression. The objective of this cartoon is obviously to highlight the pathetic plight of this lonely creature. Here is a man (the artist is saying) who has manifestly failed his Queen, his Country and Himself. He should have been out there with the rest of them committing matrimony and procreating away, so that come Christmas time he would be surrounded by lisping hordes of future Governors of New South Wales, Princes of Commerce and Raisers of Fallen Women, all tugging at his coat tails and withing (sorry, wishing) Dear Papa a Happy Christmas.

I have never gone along with the authorized interpretation of this picture and I suggest that it is worthy of closer investigation and analysis. That is a pretty good sort of bird the chap has before him on the table. There are all sorts of goodies neatly endished to go with it, so we may infer that the Bachelor has not scratched up this substantial repast himself. There is almost certainly a cook and ancillary staff behind the scenes somewhere, who are even now keeping a watchful eye on the master's plum pudding.

I think that we can assume that the decanter on the table contains a drop of the right stuff and that the entire contents is destined for the Bachelor: all except the glass or two that his man has already taken out — just to make sure that the stuff was up to the Master's high standards. I would not mind betting that out of frame to the right there is a decanter of decent vintage port waiting its turn.

Look beyond the table and there is a good fire roaring away in the grate and beside it what looks like an especially slothful armchair. It is my opinion that our Bachelor has every intention of loosening a post-prandial button or two and settling down with his feet on the fender and Mr Gibbon's latest 'damned, great, thick book' – a very definite snooze inducer – on his lap. All in all, I reckon that the mournful expression is a bit of licence on the part of the artist.

You may infer from all this that I take a fairly misanthropic view of Christmas. I have absolutely no objection to people celebrating the putative birthday of Christ: it is meet, right and the bounden duty of believers so to do.

For a great number of people, however, Christmas has nothing to do with Christianity. Christmas has reverted to the old pagan midwinter festival on which the Christian feast was so rudely grafted. It is now a broad excuse for greed, sloth, lust and insobriety. Should any member of the Church of England wish to take issue with my analysis, let him (or her) first ask himself to what extent the Church is responsible for the debasement of traditional belief. The modern Church offers drip-dry values and synthetic fibre religion when its people want the reassurance of spiritual broadcloth. Here endeth the sermon.

Be that as it may, my reasons for disliking Christmas are mainly commercial and social.

The other day I telephoned a certain firm about an item of agricultural equipment which I wanted as quickly as possible. The spokesman of the firm sucked his teeth and, with the ill concealed glee of an Englishman telling another Englishman that he cannot have what he wants, told me that delivery was unlikely before the end of January: the factory in question was shut for three weeks over Christmas and the New Year.

After the initial flush of annoyance, one appreciates the soundness of this management decision. The Management knows that the Great British Workforce is going to be out of its collective skull and off its legs for the duration of the festivities: it might just be up to holding its head and moaning feebly: it certainly will not be up to bolting widgets onto doofers.

I suppose that I resent this semi-national flake-out because I have to work on Christmas Day, New Year's Day, and Uncle Tom Cobbleigh's day as well, as do all others who have to tend stock. It says a lot for the stamina of the countryman that one seldom hears of cases of neglect induced by over indulgence. The sheep may be fed a little later on Christmas morning; the cows may have to wait a bit for their breakfast after Old Year's Night. There may be a slight problem adjusting the vision for a correct count of the lambs on the baigies. But the jobs will be done.

I do remember hearing of one ex-shepherd who felt unable to face a wet and windy morning (after a particularly wet and windy night in the Drovers' Arms). He told his wife to run the hose pipe over his oilskins and wellingtons and leave them outside the door for the boss to see, whilst he buried his head under the blankets. He forgot to tell her to wet the collie dogs as well. As I said, he is an ex-shepherd.

In fact I do not really mind working at Christmas. It allows me to escape from that Christmas horrow show: the Family Gathering.

Yes, yes, I know that one should rejoice in the presence of the family, but you have not seen my family. Every year they descend upon us by the charabanc load — aunts, uncles, cousins, brothers, sisters-in-law. My wife stoutly maintains that she knows who they all are, but I do wonder sometimes. There was the pint-sized chap who came and ate for two one year. My wife said that it was my Uncle Sidney. I do not have an Uncle Sidney. I think that Christmas will have to become a 'tickets only' do. The problem is that my idea of fast living is my pipe, a book and my armchair.

The pipe has been confiscated for the duration of Aunt Emma's stay.

The Brother has gone to ground in the loo with the book.

The armchair seethes with relations I have never knowingly seen before.

However, relief is at hand: I can invent some urgent bit of stockmanship which enables me to weasel out of compulsory family jollity. The sheep have got to be fed. Then the dogs and I can go to the top of the farm and watch the frosty sun going down over the hills – and, oh joy, I just happen to find a spare pipe in my jacket pocket.

Should the hills be concealed by a blizzard, we can go and sit in the shed and watch the sleet drive by: it must be better than Christmas television.

I think that the *Punch* Batchelor had really cracked Christmas.

Chapter Forty-Five

A DAY AT
CLONMEL RACES

THE POPULATION OF the Republic of Ireland is approximately 3.5 million, which is also approximately the size of
the population of Birmingham. To the best of my knowledge
and belief the solid Burghers of Birmingham do not have a
single racecourse to their credit. The punters of Eire can
choose from twenty-six. These statistics may give some idea
of the position that the horse holds in Irish Society. You may
remember that the Celts worshipped a horse goddess called
Epona (now you know whence the word 'pony' comes) and, I
do not think that the cult has ever completely died out in
Ireland. The horse looms large across the waters — but not
all loom as large as the one I met in Limerick City.

It was pitch dark and raining (as sometimes happens in
Ireland) and I was driving in an orderly manner and a n.
easterly direction along the Limerick ring road, when I met a
horse galloping towards me. It was being ridden (bareback) by
two long-haired youths. I just had time to notice all this as the
horse flashed by me. I have never been to Selly Oaks but I
suspect that that sort of thing rarely happens there.

I do not suppose that a galloping horse would raise many
eyebrows in Clonmel.

It is just possible that there are those amongst you who
have never heard of Clonmel (Cluain Meala: the Field of
Honey) and are wondering where it is. It is a nice quiet little
market town (pop: c.11,000) that lies at the foot of the
Comeragh Mountains. It is 9 miles from Fethard; 10 from
Cahir and 13 from Carrick on Suir: you see, you knew where

it was all the time. The racecourse lies just to the north of the town, in what remains of Powerstown Park. The most previous racecourse I had been on was Churchill Downs, Kentucky. American racing is very boring, but you are bored in great comfort. You do not go to Clonmel to be bored, and the amenities are practicable. Except for the Gents. Entrance and exit is through the same straitened door. I got badly trampled by a priest in this door; no doubt his need was greater than mine.

It is a neat little oval course on a slope up from the stands which makes for good viewing. The Experts (all 3.5 million of them) tell me that it is, in fact, plenty tight enough from the horse/jockey angle and that you do not take your best horse there. However, it is not like the course I was told about where the jockeys had gone on strike the week before and had refused to ride until the authorities got a chain saw and tidied up a couple of the fences.

It seemed that the tactful thing to do would be to have a word with the Racecourse Secretary and let him know what great joy was being bestowed upon him by my presence. I got lots of helpful (and totally conflicting) suggestions as to where he might be found. His lair was located at last. Clonmel keeps its Racecourse Secretary in a little green tin shed somewhere down the back of the stands. It appeared to be windowless and the door was heavily padlocked. I never quite established whether they had him locked inside, or whether he had pocketed the key and decided to do what I decided to do: have a large Paddy (a brand of whiskey, in case you are wondering) and water. So next to the Club Stand.

All this talk of club stands might just give an impression of exclusivity: flower beds, Old Etonians chucking bread rolls at each other, gleaming paint work, popping champagne corks, and men in bowler hats stopping you coming in if your skirts are too short.

Clonmel is not really like that. For one thing, if you do not have a ticket, you just pop round the corner and buy one for a quid at the kiosk. It is an odd kiosk. It looks like one of those concrete coal bunkers. There is someone in it, because a hand comes out of a hole and takes your money and hands out a badge. I just could not see how they got the person (presumably very small) attached to the hand in and out.

The gate of the Club Stand is manned by large jovial chaps who, quite rightly, insist on seeing your ticket and refusing you entry if you do not have one. This is quite right and proper, but there would be more point to it if there was not a perfectly good side entrance which was not guarded at all.

There were several lady jockeys on the card. From my vantage point in the stand, it was plain to see that one of them was having trouble with the Lady Jockeys' Changing-room: at least, that is what I assume it must have been. It looked more like the place where the lawn mower would normally be stabled, but then she would hardly have been so keen to get in there. She could not open the door. She turned the handle: nothing. She shook the handle: nothing. She put down her bag and kicked the door: the door stood firm. If she then really said what one thinks she said, then one must be profoundly shocked. This mini drama had collected a small crowd of interested spectators. Two of them took some sort of marker post out of the ground and began to batter the door with it. It availed them nothing. It was a bit worrying too, because from where I sat it did rather look as though that door might be holding up the stand above it. Both the lady and the crowd were getting excited but then a man appeared with a key, the door surrendered at last and the stand remained standing. I reckoned that the lady's adrenaline had been nicely pumped up. Indeed, this seems to have been the case for she rode a tremendous finish in the second race, being just beaten by half a length.

Clonmel is a small racecourse deep in the country and the meeting was on a Thursday. In spite of this, there seemed to be a very fair crowd there. The crowd may have been helped by the fact that the early part of the week had been taken up by the big coursing meeting, which also happens on the racecourse. This event brings thousands of people from all over Ireland and Britain, some of whom had undoubtedly stayed on for the races. They reckon that the four-day coursing meeting is worth two million Irish pounds to Clonmel.

Greyhounds are next to horses in Irish animal hagiology

and the most famous of all greyhounds was master M'Grath. This amazing dog won the Waterloo Cup (coursing's Cup Final) in 1868, 1869 and 1871. There is a large memorial to him in the Club Stand; the original, in Dungarvan, Co Waterford was 'defaced by opponents of Field Sports in 1985'. Ireland, too, has its Loony Left. I do not think there would be much left of any loony who tried a bit of defacing at Clonmel.

I am not a great betting man but I know a good thing when I see one. I turned a deaf ear to 'The Lady' (my guide and mentor for the occasion) burbling on about form and fetlocks and 'staying the trip'; what was needed was inspiration, intuition. So I had a modest wager on Ms Lulu Ollyfut in the second. Ms Ollyfut is a splendid Scandinavian lady, built on proper Brunhildean lines, who is well thought of in Irish racing circles. Ollyfut is not her real name but it is the nearest the Irish can get to pronouncing it. As I said, I know a good thing when I see one. I could not see her hocks, but by golly she looked a stayer. She came in fifth. Ah well.

It hardly needs saying that the crowd contained a large number of priests. Irish priests are heavily into horses and country sports and quite right too. The Church of England would be a better place if our own pallid prelates took in more fresh air and exercise; cleanse their minds of unhealthy obsessions, I should not wonder. However, I really do think that the Cardinal Archbishop should have a word with his chaps about hats. I mean, they always used to wear those black trilbys but now it is bobble hats and baseball caps: perhaps it is something to do with Vatican 2.

For the fourth race, I walked out into the country leaving the roar and jostle of the stands behind me. It was a day of extraordinary springlike weather. Had it been May it would have been just right; for the second of February, it was ridiculous. I leant on a rail and lit my pipe and looked at the great sweep of the brown Comeraghs rising above the town, smelt the faint reek of the turf smoke and felt 'the peace come dropping slow'. It was a good moment. But I do not want you to think that I was out there to footle about. There was a purpose. I was about my masters' business.

Between the third and second furlong markers, the course makes a pretty tight bend before coming into the home straight and I reasoned that this was a pressure point and a good place for collecting the *obiter dicta* of the passing jockeys. This indeed proved to be the case. There are some very interesting entries in my notebook, but they are not such as I feel justified in putting on general release.

One memory abides, however, of a bunch of horses coming hard round the turn, with one chap well boxed in on the rails and his heartfelt cry of: 'Jasus! Yese have me murthered altogether!'

It was time to return to the seething crowds and to look and listen.

'Tim! Did ye get the winner?'

'I did. I had seven pounds on him. Now that's a gamble.'

'Fair does to ye, Tim boy.'

The imperious and compelling cry of 'The Lady' shattered my musing. I was being summoned to meet the 'Clonmel Racegoers Supporters' Club'. This happy band of pilgrims have a nice club room tucked away upstairs: it used to be the Members' Stand in the days when there were such things.

My first reaction was: what a very nice lot of people and: what a pity that I had not strayed upon their lair earlier on. Subsequent events and the wisdom of hindsight, however, suggest that it was probably just as well that I did not find them any earlier.

The course of the remainder of the afternoon can be traced through the gradual collapse of my carefully kept notes from untidiness, through illegibility, to total incoherence and finally blank-paged oblivion. You see, they are all such very charming people and they all had that wonderful Irish gift of making one feel that one was the best thing since drisheen (black pudding), fried eggs and soda bread. The highest honour they could aspire to in life, it seemed, was to buy one drinks. When I say 'one drinks', I mean that they bought one several drinks; or even rather a lot of drinks. Any offer by the Saxon to pay for a drink was greeted with cries of Celtic Horror.

I am ashamed to say that I cannot remember the names of everybody I met, but I do remember the impressive and genial bulk of Jerry Chalke (a publican). There was Eddie Hickey the baker, with whom I shared a mutual interest in keeping sheep and a mutual hope that one day they would begin to keep us. I remember Noel Davern and his wife Marie. Noel is the local TD (Member of Parliament) and is entirely sound on Field Sports, Farm Support, the Proper Growth of a Property-owning Democracy, Europe and Buying Whiskey. I wish he was my MP.

I cannot leave Clonmel without mentioning Eileen Kiely, secretary of the Supporters' Club and a high official of the Bank of Ireland. I had just negotiated a massive overdraft with the Bank of Ireland when 'The Lady' and my wife appeared and, taking an ear each, led me away to the car.

I am not really a racing man, within the meaning of the act, but I did enjoy Clonmel. Clonmel is different, and I left the racecourse thinking that the world was a better place than it was when I arrived.

Master McGrath

Chapter Forty-Six

WILDLIFE
IN A FRENCH
FOREST

THE LIONS VERY nearly disturbed my luncheon. This would have been a pity as it was quite one of the best luncheons that I can remember: a positive *gastronomique* milestone along the alimentary way of life.

I had returned to central France to renew my love affair with the great oak forests that are such a feature of that part of the country. There is nothing that I know of in Britain that compares with these beautiful woods which still cover many thousands of acres, or (if you insist) hectares.

Some of the forests are state-owned but many are still in private (very) hands. Whatever, they are still managed in an ancient and very successful way. This management system is best explained by starting at the end, when the great oaks are finally felled (for this is a commercial operation).

The oaks are allowed to regenerate, so that the clearing eventually becomes an area of oak saplings. When these reach a certain stage of growth, the coppice is thinned out leaving the better specimens with space about them. This space is then planted with beech. The beech saplings, being faster growing, force the young oaks to reach upwards to the sun, therefore insuring that they grow with a beautiful straight trunk.

The next stage is the eventual cutting of the beech which is corded and sold for fire wood.

The oaks, straight as gun barrels, are then left to grow and mature until, aged circa 150, they are judged to be ripe for felling.

The whole process then begins all over again.

This is man working with and for nature. The forests that are produced by this method produce good quality timber. They also provide a marvellous natural habitat for beasts, birds and insects of all descriptions.

I could also say that these amazing woods provide spiritual food for the souls of men scarred and soured by materialistic mayhem. But a chap cannot go about saying that sort of thing: it is just not British, but then neither, sadly, are the forests.

But where, I hear you cry, are the lions? Are they too creeping about the oak woods feasting on pâté-proud picnickers? Well, no, not really.

My hostess, having struck a day when there was no hunting to be found within a hundred miles, took me to luncheon with a friend.

Madame Huberte Villenave is the current sprig (and I hope she will excuse the expression) on the ancient tree of Rolland d'Arbouire. The family have lived at the Château de St Augustin since the time of the first acorn. Madame wore black throughout 1989 as a protest against the Revolution.

Madame Huberte is very fond of animals and so it was quite natural for her to start a wildlife park. It is quite one of the best managed wildlife parks that I have seen, with a vet as *directeur*. The animals look well and contented and Madame Huberte has a quite extraordinary rapport with them. You need quite a lot of rapport to kiss a tiger.

In front of the château is a great semicircular courtyard and here be lions. It is a bit startling, at first, to have lions jumping up at the window during luncheon: makes a chap spill things down his shirt front, but after a bit one takes it for granted and discounts the suggestion that an English *maitre d'équipage* might make an interesting change to the lions' diet.

After lunch we toured the wildlife park, but the greatest pleasure for me was when we were taken into the private forest. Madame Huberte has one thousand hectares of oak forest. In the back of the car was a dustbin full of stale bread. From time to time we would stop and get out.

'Ki – Ki – Ki – Ki' Madame Huberte warbled, casting her bits of bread about and soon there was movement and dark shapes appeared amongst the trees. The wild boar were coming: big ones, small ones, they scuffled and fought and squealed for the tit bits. But they are truly wild and only really used to the proprietor. The slightest strange movement and they are off.

In the middle of the forest is a little cottage where the family stay during the red deer rut, and we saw a herd of deer grazing nearby.

Madame Huberte is a fascinating person: a mad keen hunter and a passionate naturalist. Next time you are in France you should not miss a chance of visiting the Château de St Augustin at Château-sur-Allier, 03320 Lurcy-Levis.

Chapter Forty-Seven

MEETING THE MAPAHOLICS

I HAVE ALWAYS BEEN fascinated by maps. I can occasionally snatch a few spare moments from the importunities of sheep, wives and editors: I am happy to spend such precious time curled up with a map trying to work out the best way from Rhiconich to Tongue. In case you should seek my advice on this one, it is to go by Achfary and Meallan Liath Coire Mhic Dhughaill; do not forget to turn left after Colaboll.

Come, let us twist through the lanes and tracks; up hill, down dale and then get thoroughly stuck up the wheel hubs in that blasted re-entrant.

Could I, do you suppose, really manage to puff up all those contour lines to the top of Fan-Gihirych and would I be able to pronounce it any better if I did?

Some of the place names are very evocative. I know what happened at Skirle Naked (Scots retreating from Flodden stripped off to ford the river, then performed a reel or two to get dry. It did not do them much good. The English caught them at Bloodybush Edge) but I wonder what dark deed happened at Murder Cleugh. Then there is the matter of the strange proximity of the Copper Snout to the Lord's Seat.

All these names and much interesting information may be gleaned from the maps of the Ordnance Survey. But who and what is it; and why? I have to confess that I would not have been able to answer any of those questions a short time ago. Now I know more.

The Ordnance Survey came into my life because I had to tackle them about a glaring omission on one of their maps. I am not now talking about that pathetic Welsh mountain that everybody got so excited about. Anyway, as I understand it, the mountain was quite clearly marked; it was just that no one had got around to giving it a name — and did it matter, anyway? No, I am talking about something much more important. An entire farmhouse was missing from the map: My Farmhouse.

In 1984 I bought a block of land. On this 'Zero Development Base' I built — as you will know if you started this book at the beginning — a large shed for housing my sheep and a little house for housing me and mine. It is a neat snug little steading with stunning views across the Cheviot Hills, and it is called Breamish Parks. It did not appear on any map. I felt aggrieved so packed up my grievance and took it to the Ordnance Survey.

The next problem for me was to find this shadowy and probably rather sinister organization.

You find them in the telephone book.

Some two hundred years ago, the Board of Ordnance, who were mainly concerned with artillery, were given the task of providing accurate maps of the south coast of England. The idea was that if Napoleon shoved his nasty little nose into, say, Newhaven, then our gallant lads would know which way to go to see him off. The invasion menace disappeared but the demand for mapping remained and burgeoned.

The Ordnance Survey became a separate government department. There it remains today, although it is a loosely-bound liegeman of the Department of the Environment.

The headquarters of the Ordnance Survey is in Southampton, but that is for later. For now you will have to accompany my complaint and me to Alnwick where the local survey team hangs its collective hat. There I discovered Neil Tomas (sic). Neil is a Mapping and Charting Officer. MCOs are the men who actually go out in all sorts of wind and weather and work where all maps start: on the ground.

The maintenance of maps is a question of constant revision. It is obvious that some areas need revising more often than others. Information flows in from the Local Authorities, the Public Utilities, and the Great British Public, but a great deal of information simply comes from the local officers knowing their patch and just keeping their eyes open. Very broadly put, when there is enough survey work to justify a day's work in an area, then it is surveyed. The re-survey of Breamish Parks fitted neatly into this slot.

One of the many nice things about the Ordnance Survey is the enthusiasm of its staff members for their maps. Neil is a typical map man. He is in his thirties, and joined the OS straight from school. After training, he spent his early years working all over Scotland and the Islands. He has now worked at Alnwick for four years, which suits him well as he is a local man.

On the appointed morning he appeared at the farm, slung about with map boards, tape measures, and enthusiasm. I had rather expected theodolites and a pile of complicated measuring equipment. This was not to be. The basic mapping equipment consists of a tape measure and a stout pair of boots. So that was the first stage: tramping through the thistles, measuring every length and angle, making copious notes and continuously checking everything with the existing map. It would be more correct to say maps because, just to make things more interesting, the farm covers the corners of four maps. Neil's enthusiasm overcame all obstacles.

From Field to Office. In the Alnwick office, I met the MSD. Like all large organisations, the Ordnance Survey have a verbal shorthand and are very prone to talk to each other in initials. The Master Survey Document is the definitive 1:2500 sheet from which all other sheets spring. The results of the Field Survey are drawn onto the MSD in pencil. When the surveyor is satisfied, the alterations are completed in black ink and annotations are added. For instance, there are three CGs (cattle grids) on my farm road. I have put in a dipping system which appears as 'Sheep Dip'. Local custom is always used for annotations; in some parts of the country my dipper would appear as a 'Sheep Wash'.

The next stage of the mapping is for the revised MSD to be sent to the Group Office in Newcastle-upon-Tyne for approval by the Chief Surveyor. Let us accompany it thither.

Iain Thomas is the Chief Surveyor. He introduced me to that interesting couple SUSI and SIM.

SUSI was made immediately available to me.

Once the MSD has been thoroughly checked, the information thereon is immediately available to the GBP (Great British Public: this sort of thing is catching) through the Supply of Updated/Unpublished Survey Information. You can get paper copies/transparent film copies/enlargements on film to a different map scale.

Iain sat me down with a cup of coffee. Twenty minutes later I was presented with a copy of the updated map complete with Breamish Parks; and that you might think is the end of the story. You should get so lucky.

There is still SIM.

SIM does not live with SUSI. Survey Information on or from Microfilm gets supplied from Southampton. That is where the MSD goes to be copied onto microfilm and that is where we should go next.

The headquarters of the Ordnance Survey in Southampton is massive complex of buildings where some two thousand people stack their briefcases. Complex is indeed the word; it would be an easy building to get lost in, but not when you have Wendy Fellingham as guide and mentor. Wendy is the IPO (Information and Press Officer). All doors open for her, all paths become smooth; the strait becomes broad. She is a positive human dynamo generating energy and enthusiasm. Enthusiasm could well be the Ordnance Survey motto.

You really cannot *do* the Southampton HQ in one day. You especially cannot do it if you are a STA (Slow-Thinking Agriculturalist) with a limited grasp of matters technical. Wendy had mapped out a comprehensive tour for me. Everyone I met stopped being very busy to make me welcome. But I was undone by enthusiasm. Light my touch paper on foxhunting or sheep and I will fizz, crackle and pop for hours. I saw the same glow kindle in the eyes of the ladies and gentlemen of the Ordnance Survey when they were invited to enlarge on their specialities.

Now please do not expect me to explain all the intricate technical details of map making to you. I should get in a muddle. Everybody would get cross with me. There would be blood (mine) on the carpet. Let me tell you my impressions instead.

It is obvious that the making of maps is a way of life; not just a job. The Map Makers love their work and are always trying to find ways to improve it. For example, in the Survey Department at Southampton they have an amazing plotting machine that allows two men to do the work that was once done by forty manual draughtsmen. There always had to be at least one draughtsman who was 6'6' tall (this is absolutely kosher) because shorter men could not work on the maps in the middle of the table. Work ground to a halt if the tall man was off sick. The present plotting machine cost £100,000 but it and its attendant computer software were developed in-house. After all, as one man very reasonably pointed out, no one is going to know what computer programmes will suit the Ordnance Survey better than the Ordnance Survey people themselves.

I am intimidated by large pieces of machinery and I felt suitably humbled on the Print Floor where all sorts and conditions of maps are printed. The presses appeared huge and each one seemed to have an overalled bottom sticking out of its entrails. My head (and our guide) told me that these were highly-skilled technicians making highly-skilled adjustments to delicate machinery. My fevered imagination suggested that they were in fact part of the daily sacrifice required by the machines: Map-making Molochs.

Next there were huge guillotines which chopped great piles of maps into the required sizes. There were machines for folding maps into the sizes convenient for putting in your pocket. There was a machine called Hunkeler, which sounds like a new brand of lager. In fact, it is an amazingly complex machine that puts the covers on maps, so that when you put them in your pocket you do not get them stuck together with bits of old toffee.

Then there was Digitizing.

Digitizing is a rather dreadful word for a very interesting and useful process. It is officially described as: 'The representation of conventional map detail (lines, points and text) in a form suitable for manipulation by computer. The Ordnance Survey converts this map detail into strings of co-ordinates on magnetic tape.' I really do not think that I could have explained it better myself, but if you really want to wallow in the technical depths of this process, then you should ask the Ordnance Survey for their Information Pack. Any further attempt at explanation by me might end in Idiotizing the whole thing. In the next few years, the whole country will be digitized and you will not feel a thing.

So what is the practical application of this? Do you remember my telling you that four different map sheets came together on my farm? Quite obviously this can be a nuisance. Once this area is digitized there will be no more rigid cartographical boundaries. The OS will be able to lift a complete map of my farm (or any other given area) out of the computer and supply it to me on one sheet. Not only that but the map could be tailor-made to show only specific topographical features. Suppose, for example, that I wanted a map that showed just the fence lines on the farm and nothing else at all. This would present no problem. You do not have to be a highly-skilled surveyor to understand all the possible applications of this system.

There is a whole mass of goodies which will come spilling out of the basket of digitization. Those in-car family rows that flame up over 'someone's' inability to read maps will become a thing of the past. The Butcher, Baker, and the Man-Who-Ought-To-Know-How-To-Mend-The-Washing-Machine-But-Never-Does will no longer have to scratch their heads to find Acacia Avenue. We shall all have In-Car Navigation Systems which will guide us on our journey from start to finish. You think I jest? Such a system already exists and will be generally available soon: at a price. In ten years' time, they will be as common as home computers.

There is much more to tell and not space enough to tell it. The Ordnance Survey will be only to pleased to show and tell you themselves. Five thousand visitors are welcomed at Southampton every year, but only by *prior arrangement*, please. Write to The Public Relations Department, Ordnance Survey, Romsey Road, Southampton SO9 4DH.

You will find it on the map; just like Breamish Parks.

Chapter Forty-Eight

THE STRAINS AND PAINS OF COUNTRY LIVING

'You know,' said Jimmy, 'it was that funny that even if you had been killed we would still have had to laugh.'

The occasion for this merriment was a spectacular fall performed by myself. I do not suppose that you have much interest in the matter but I am going to tell you just the same.

I had been proceeding along the side of a steep hill on my four-wheeled bike when I hit a concealed rock. The bike turned bustle over apex and catapulated me into space, where I spread my arms like Superman, soared down the hill and did an emergency landing in a patch of bracken. The bike (which weighs a quarter of a ton) was obviously desolate at having let the side down and and came rolling down the hill to settle confidentally on top of me.

Jimmy had been leaning on the stone dyke at the bottom of the hill and stayed there choking on his pipe and roaring with laughter. Other men whose senses of humour were less sophisticated came and extracted me.

Odd bits were bent and dented and the bike was a bit bruised as well, but no great harm was done. Indeed, I have been extremely lucky over the years, especially when you consider my propensity for falling off horses. I have been rolled on, jumped on, fallen with, kicked, catapulated head first into a blackthorn hedge; have been upside in a water-filled rhyne with a horse upside down on top of me. Praise the Lord, in all the years when I was falling off horses, I never had a serious injury. To the best of my knowledge and belief, I only lost three days' hunting in thirty years: once with influenza, once after a more than usually comprehensive squashing and once as a result of being left dangling by one leg from a gatepost (knee twisted like a dish cloth: definitely not recommended). Oh yes, and I broke my collar bone when I was ten, but everybody does that so it does not count.

Rural life and work is still fairly physical. Pains, strains, and mangled appendages are regarded pretty much as a matter of course. I am at this moment suffering from a strained back: the result of unloading a lorry-load of hay without due care and attention. For those of you who like facts and figures, a hay bale weights approximately 45 lbs and there are about 360 bales on a lorry load.

So I am feeling sorry for myself, but I am in a better state than the poor chap who was suffering from 'a Twisted Pot and an Ebenezer Ulcer'. Twisted Pots are probably ecumenical, but I have always assumed that Ebenezer Ulcers are reserved for Non-Conformists and are very likely connected with stewed tea.

Arthritis and rheumatic problems are rife in rural areas as a result of continuous and prolonged exposure to the elements. Doctors will speak severely about getting wet and then allowing the clothes to dry on the person. This is all very fine but supposing you are 2000 feet up and ten miles from anywhere? so we get wet and cold and eventually get the twingeing screws. Mind you, these things can be taken to excess.

There was an old man who was bent double when I knew him. As a young man he would ride to the hill every day to look at the sheep. He often returned home wet through, and it was then his custom to stand in front of the open range in the kitchen and turn himself round and round (in a cloud of steam) until dry.

He would never wear a waterproof coat, and here I am with him most definitely. I have yet to discover a coat that keeps the wet out without keeping the condensation in. The same thing applies to rubber boots. In fact, I am not really into rubber at all, although there was one occasion when I stretched a point.

I had chopped half way through a finger with a bill hook.

The hospital stitched, sewed, bandaged and splinted the finger. They then sent me away with stern instructions not to get it wet. How then was I to go hunting and keep my finger dry? I needed some sort of tough, durable, waterproof covering that would neatly fit over a splinted finger.

You will have guessed the answer. I expect you used them in the Army, for keeping your rifle barrel dry.

Chapter Forty-Nine

BUREAUCRATIC MADNESS

I VOTED TO JOIN the Common Market; just that. I am in favour of fewer restrictions on trade. I want to sell my lambs dearly to the French and pay less for the wine. I did not vote (absolutely not) to become a Citizen of a United States of Europe. I certainly did not vote to burden myself with yet another layer of bureaucracy. Nor do I wish to finance more politicians in their in-depth researches into their research assistants. However, there is an aspect of Europeanism that I find even more worrying: the apparent fanaticism of its devotees. Those who favour the concept of a United Europe seem to be remarkably intolerant of the views of those of us who dissent.

The protagonists of Europeanism seem to regard their cause as something sacred. They cannot conceive that any rational person might not support all their aims. They therefore reason that any resistance to their ideas is irrational, immoral and offensive. These enthusiasts think that Europeanism should be everybody's ideal, must be the only truth and will be good for us whether we like it or not. This is a dangerous thought path. History has shown us that all 'isms and 'ologies are to be mistrusted. Communism and National Socialism started as ideals and turned into Auschwitz and Kolyma. I am all for people having ideals just as long as they resist the urge to put them into practice and frighten the horses. An ideal imposed on others ceases to be an ideal.

I try to avoid flying British Airways whenever possible. Lord

King has yet to make his minions conscious of the fact that they are actually running a service for paying customers, not a detention centre. British Airways' motto could well be: 'Nanny knows best'. I resent being addressed as 'Passenger Poole' and generally being treated as though I had an IQ of 25. Most of all I resent this 'No Smoking' nonsense. I do not actually want to smoke when flying, but I do want to pay my money and take my choice.

Air France has grubby loos but a more human approach. Smoking is important to my wife, especially when flying. We flew to Paris recently and only 'No Smoking' seats were available.

We consulted the Steward. He shrugged: 'It is only a leetle bit forbidden,' he said.

Interested in Endangered Species?

Anguished by the plight of Persecuted Minorities?

Of course, you are.

Right then; clock the picture on the right and you will see a prime example of both.

I am an Ab Origine Countryman.

We Abos make up only about three percent of the British population and Urban Man (the other ninety-seven percent) is out to get us. Urban Man thinks that it is high time that the countryside was sanitized, pasteurized, civilized and, well, urbanized. It had better be homogenized in time for 1992 as well.

The trouble lies in the fact that every Urban Man loves the country and wants to re-establish his rural roots. But he is disappointed to find that the countryside is not as it should be. The countryside is dirty, muddy and smelly. It has rebellious septic tanks and unlit roads where one might be mugged by a sheep.

Urban Man reckons that all this is the fault of the indigenous inhabitants who wear the wrong coloured wellies and seem to spend a lot of time farming and killing things. Urban Man knows that there is no point in farming because he can buy all the food he wants in the supermarket. He knows that hunting and shooting are wrong because someone who lives in Hampstead told him so. Therefore, it follows that the people who pursue this anachronistic way of life must also be Pointless and Wrong and something should be done about them.

I am one of the Pointless and Wrong and that is why I am feeling Persecuted and Endangered. It is possible that we Aborigines feel rather as the Sioux must have felt when they topped that frightful chap, Custer: we may be on our way to the dustbin of history, but there might be a Little Big Horn first.

Chapter Fifty

'BEST RIDING
BY MOONLIGHT'

A s soon as I took my thermos out of the bait bag it started to snow. The northerly gale gave the snow a certain venomous force. If you live my sort of life you get resigned to the Clerk of the Weather getting in a snit and dumping things on you. You certainly do not allow it to upset something important like luncheon. I just moved myself into the lee of the ruined house and sat stolidly chomping my soggy sandwiches whilst the snowflakes whirled about me and a fragment of door banged drearily in the wind.

There is a great sadness about a ruined house and you have to be pretty dull of soul not to have a bit of a wonder about all the people who have lived, laughed, loved, cried and died in such a place. It is a lonely spot now. How much more lonely it must have been in the days of horse, cart and Shank's pony.

The nearest tiny hamlet is six miles by the crow and rather further by man. The nearest thing to a service in the old days would have been the weekly visit of the carrier's cart to a spot three miles down the valley. This would have been the highlight of the week for the inhabitants of the the isolated steading.

Yet generations of people lived and worked in that old steading well into living memory. They were indeed 'hard and heather bred' for the steading stands 1500 feet up and is attacked by every wind that blows. The weak and sickly would die; the rest would grow strong on a diet of milk, barley porridge and fat bacon and the fact that whichever way they went they would have to walk down and conversely up a 1 in 4 hill.

The date on the lintel of the house is 1819, but I suspect that there would have been other houses on the site before that because it sits beside one of the old roads across the border.

Now you may think that the only road that crosses the English/Scottish Border and the Cheviot Hills is the A68 via Carter Bar and from a motor vehicular point of view you are quite right. In fact, there are many other roads: Dere Street, The Street, Clennell Street, The Salters' Road and The Thieves' Road – these were all trunk roads in their day. They were the old drove roads, the ancient green roads down which thousands of cattle and sheep would have made their way to southern markets.

They are slumbering now these old roads, seen only by shepherds, walkers and occasional squads of sweating soldiery who never look to me as though they are enjoying the beauty of their surroundings. ('Come on, come on – it's only pain!')

In other days, the old roads would have seen plenty of warlike activity. These were the roads the reivers used in the bloody days of the border raids.

For several centuries, up to the Union of England and Scotland, doing it to the other side before they did it unto you was the only form of regular employment on the border. Cattle lifting was the main industry with Murder, Rape and Pillage as the by-products. I cannot think that it was a merry life and it was usually a short one but undoubtedly profitable. It is salutary to remember that many respected and noble border families laid the foundations of their fortunes by stealing cattle and slitting throats: entrepreneurial skills, I suppose.

'Best riding by moonlight' was the motto of one of the famous riding clans. The full moons of the early winter (when the granaries were full and the cattle fit) was the favourite time for raiding: it became known as the 'Reivers' Moon'. I was coming down past the deserted house by the light of a full November moon one night. Once past the house, the old road drops down into a steep sided valley and runs beside a rushing stream. It was a still, frosty night and there was no sound except for the clink of the horses' hooves on the stony track echoing in the night, and the prattling of the stream. Moonlight and echo can have funny effects. It did sound as though there was more than one horse in the valley. I suppose that the moon-thrown shadow of a hunting cap could look a bit like a 'steel bonnet', but how did it happen that my shadow seemed to have a lance over its shoulder? Funny thing, moonlight.

Now there was nothing funny coming down the ancient track whilst I was eating my sandwiches except snow, so I packed up my bag, tipped my hat to the old house and its memories and set off down the road towards home.

Chapter Fifty-One

A SLICE
OF THE HILLS

I HAVE JUST SPENT a day amongst the Grousers.
Perhaps you think that I should be more specific. Very well:
I attended the Northumberland Grouse Seminar which was
organized in conjunction with the Scottish Grouse Research
Project.

There were some 112 people crammed into a village hall.
Of them, 111 were landowners, shoot organizers and gamekeepers. The 112th was me, who has never shot a grouse and
who has never even met one that it was possible to get a fork
into.

However, I have no objection to other people shooting
things, always provided that their activities do not interfere
with my hunting. Sometimes they do. The problems that at
times arise between hunting and shooting are all part of a
much larger problem: more people wanting to do more things
in a countryside that is rapidly shrinking. It is the old quart
and pint pot situation and it means the hills are suffering.

I have always liked the hills and the wilder parts of Britain,
mainly because for most my life no one else has been much
interested in them, except for those who farmed them and
hunted in them. Times have changed and the hills and all the
rest of the countryside are under pressure. This pressure is
making all the interested parties a bit snarly and dog-in-a-
mangerish. The trouble is that all the interested parties want
something different out of poor old England and none of them
wants to listen to the other chap. There seems to be more
confrontation than consultation at the moment and this is a pity.

Nearly all the hills are privately owned. The more traditional landowner tends to growl that it is his land and he will do what he damn well likes with it. But I know (and the thinking and politically-aware magnate also knows) that this attitude will no longer wash. The landowners are going to have to bend with the breeze if it is not to become a gale and break things.

Faulty attitudes are by no means confined to the landowners. The 'Access as of Right' Lobby is becoming increasingly strident, belligerent and unreceptive to reasonable argument. I can quite understand the desire of Urban Man to look to the hills when he wants to recharge his spiritual batteries. Troubles arise because he tends to regard the hills as a sort of gigantic extension of Hampstead Heath where he can wander at will with dogs, children, wives, mistresses, aunts and Uncle Tom Cobbleigh and all.

The fact is that unlimited access to all hill land at all times is a complete nonsense. It takes no account of the fact that what the townsman regards as a playground is someone else's workshop. For the sheep farmer, a wall knocked down in a jolly romp, or a gate left open in gay abandon is certainly a nuisance: at certain times of year it can become a disaster.

Lambing time is a fraught and nerve-racking time anyway. The last thing any farmer wants is hoards of people and their dogs (yes, I am sure Fido only wanted to play, but the lamb is dead nonetheless) riving about (sic) all over the place.

People get very exercised about the preservation of heather moorland and quite right, too. What many people fail to understand is that the reason so much heather moorland has survived is that it is the habitat of that unique bird, the red grouse. Were it not for this fact, much of our heather uplands would have been conifered years ago.

Some of you may not approve of grouse shooting, but it is a fact of life that it is one of the few things that make parts of the uplands pay. In some remote parts, it is a major industry and source of employment. If you are prepared to take this fact on board, you will also realize that you cannot have unlimited amounts of people tramping across the factory floor when the production line is in operation.

All sorts and conditions of people also want a slice of the hills. They may all want something different, but I suggest that there is one thing that they have in common: a love of the high, wild, quiet places. Now, if we are are to preserve the peace of the hills we are not going to do it by fighting over them. It is high time that there was some concert (sic) about the future of the uplands and their use. It is meet and right that the British public should have reasonable rights of access, but the rights of those who live and work in the hills must be respected too.

Gentle Memo: I have taken to (sic)-ing because it occurs to me that some of my words may be impenetrable ruralspeak. I fear there was much bucolic mirth when, with reference to sheep in the barn, 'cuddling' was substituted for 'cudding': chewing the cud. I regret to say that rural humour may tend to be somewhat feculent.*

Note: this was included for the benefit of the *Daily Telegraph* subs.

Chapter Fifty-Two

LAMBING AT HIGH BLEAKHOPE

I'M A B—— TO stride out,' said Graham and how right he was. My little legs had to twinkle like billyho to keep anywhere near him. But then he is doing it every day, walking the hill that is: ten to twelve miles each round, twice a day, seven days a week. It is small wonder that he is fit.

So where were we and what were we doing?

I have kept sheep for some ten years, but I have always farmed 'in-bye', or on the low ground, and I've already mentioned my lambing shed next to the house. I thought that it was high time to find out how the other half lived and to see some lambing 'out-bye'.

You cannot get much more 'out-bye' than High and Low Bleakhope; they must be two of the hardest farms in England. They have their being at the top end of the Breamish Valley. They are four miles from the nearest public road, which does not amount to much anyway. The nearest shop is twelve miles away. There is no mains electricity. The road in, which was probably designed by a mountain goat, is routinely blocked by snow in the winter – and the locals will tell you that there are nine months of winter and three months of bad weather in the hills.

The two steadings lie in a Hope (blind valley) that was originally thought to be Black. The Black became Bleak and no one is arguing about it.

So who would live and work in such a place? Only very special people. It is a way of life that can never be easy but comes a bit easier if you are bred to it. The Nelsons are.

Edwin and Mary Nelson and their two sons, Graham and

Stewart, farm the two places as one holding. They are tenants on about four and a half thousand acres, which may sound impressive until you also hear that the land is mostly peat hag and bent grass. It is some of the wildest, bleakest hill country in the land. There is no alternative to sheep farming on this sort of land, and since the future of sheep farming does not look very rosy at present, pray that your livelihood does not become a political football in Brussels.

It was 0600 when I landed at High Bleakhope. It was a spring morning of sharp frost and brilliant sunshine. Twenty-four hours earlier everything had been covered in snow. Whilst I was pulling on my boots Graham got Bob and Laddie out of the kennel. Where would we sheep men be without our collie dogs? In trouble, that is where.

Graham is twenty-five, over six foot tall and as hard as a polecat. His eight hundred sheep are divided into four 'cuts': The Brigg, Outbye, Peat Moss and The Cantle. These are just the names of the hill areas which each bunch of sheep regards as home: where they are 'hiefed'.

We set away up the burn. It was still freezing hard in the valley bottom and I stuck my horn heid stick under my arm and my hands in my pockets.

We stopped in the field behind the steading to check a ewe. She had twins but had had a rough time with the second one. It had been a breech presentation and Graham had had to help her. She was still rather sore and pottery. Hill sheep are wild and self-reliant and normally lamb away quietly on their own but, when things do go wrong on the hill, the vigilance of the shepherd means the difference between life and death.

The first climb out onto The Brigg quietly got the red corpuscles multiplying and the stick was soon in play. Up, up and up we climbed, the frosty air scouring the lungs. A solitary raven croaked down at us.

Each morning Graham works round the hill tops and pushes the sheep downhill. On the evening round, he works below and pushes them up. In that way all the ground is covered and he can see exactly what has been born during the night and then during the day, coping with the problems as they arise; and they do as surely as the sparks fly upwards.

A shrill whistle. '*Hey! Hey! Hey Yows! Hey Yows!*' This got the ewes on their feet and moving quietly downhill. We watched for lambs, or ewes hanging back which would suggest a lamb concealed behind a 'bull snout' (grass tussock) or in a patch of rushes.

A pathetic bundle tried to stagger after its anxious mother. It was hooked up with a deft twist of Graham's stick, and was still wet from birth and shaky from the bitter cold of the night at 1500 feet. A quick check to see that all was well and it was restored to the anxious mother.

All was well on The Brigg. Several lambs born through the night were alive and well. 'Mr Fox', as he is known in the hills, had not been about: in fact, it is usually 'Mrs Fox' who does the lamb worrying. The really bad killers are usually barren vixens, or vixens who have lost their cubs. They kill for the killing and leave the sad little corpses scattered on the hill.

We now popped across to the Outbye. Nothing to it really: just drop down 600 feet, cross the river and a nice 1000-foot foot climb out: piece of cake. It was for Graham who veered away to the left with the long, effortless hill man's stride. I decided to cheat and go straight across: still the same climb up through the peat hags, but a good mile less.

We met again by Cardlar (oh, all right, Coldlaw) Cairn which is well named at 2000 feet up, but after that climb we were both content to pause for a moment. The wind was from Iceland but the sun was warm now and the view quite amazing. Behind us rose the great mass of Cheviot. To the right, across the valley, Cushat Law and Bloody Bush Edge and beyond them roll upon roll of purple hills disappeared into the distance. On the left, the distant sea glittered in the early sun. A lark sang above, pipits pipited and a curlew whistled overhead. A lovely place to be on such a morning, but it is not always thus. There were some nasty clouds brewing up and there was a lot of ground to cover yet.

Trouble: an old ewe stretched out in the heather, comatose. What we were looking at was a case of what some call 'Staggers' and some call 'Moss Ill' and the vets call something veterinary. In the capacious bag over Graham's shoulder there were all sorts of useful bits of kit for emergencies. Out came a bottle of Calcium Boroglutinate and a needle: about 80cc (subcutaneous) would do the job. The ewe was upended and injected. She was old and, from the state of her udder, soon to lamb. That combination had produced the problem. She would be sold off the hill into a kinder climate in the autumn. Before she was released, a hank of wool was pulled out of her fleece and knotted into the wool on the back of her head. This white tuft would stand out and mark her for future attention.

On across the still frozen peat hags (we were onto the Peat Moss now). The clefts and holes of the old peat cuttings can be death traps to weak and unwary lambs, so these areas needed special attention. There were a nice few lambs there and a new pair of twins to mark with a paint stick. All the new twins are marked so that, if he sees only one marked lamb with a ewe on a future round, Graham will know that there is one missing and institute search proceedings.

We were on The Cantle (down to a mere 1600 feet) now and scared off a dozen corbies (carrion crows). These birds are the real villains of the hills. They steal the eggs and kill the chicks of the ground-nesting birds. They peck the eyes out of weakly little lambs and even out of grown ewes if they come upon one in difficulties. They are not nice to know and yet those fools in Brussels, egged on by the Loony Grunes from Germany, want these killers protected. That is one law that I would break very firmly.

From the end of The Cantle, we looked away down the valley with the baby river Breamish glittering in the sun – but the glittering was about to stop.

The clouds that had threatened were now about to deliver. From across the valley, a ragged, hanging, grey curtain was sweeping inexorably towards us: behind us sunshine, before us snow. Such is the uncertainty of the weather in the hills.

In fact, it turned out to be hail and very nasty too, thank you very much. There was no shelter up there and there was nothing for it but to turn our backs to it, turn up the coat collar and stand it out. The dogs came and huddled miserably at our feet.

It was sharp, but mercifully short, and left the hills white with ice which glistened in the returned sun.

The Low Bleakhope steading was below us now. A distant whistling and shouting came from the far hill behind the farm. It was Stewart coming in from the round of his hill.

We turned back for High Bleakhope and started to descend The Cantle. Graham had seen two pairs of twins below us and wanted to get them into the field by the steading. The side of The Cantle is nearly vertical and was slippery. I proceeded downwards with dignity (small) and caution (great). Graham took off across the face, moving with the agility of one of his Swaledale sheep, to turn one of the ewes with twins down hill.

The dogs were patiently holding the two family units by the gate when we got to it, the ewes stamping defiantly at them. We put them through the gate and they immediately set away grazing, the lambs stotting and bouncing around them.

We had been nearly six hours on the hill.

At half past two, Graham would be setting out again and would likely be on the hill until dark.

There is not much easy living at High Bleakhope.

Chapter Fifty-Three

THE AGE-OLD CRAFT OF HEDGING

I WONDER WHEN YOU were last Cut and Laid? If it was as long ago as fifteen years then it is high time that you were done again. I am talking about your thorn hedges, of course; what else?

Cutting and laying is one of the oldest and best forms of hedge conservation and is probably as old as the thorn fences themselves. Quick thorn is the best for fences and its natural inclination is to grow straight up to the light. This is fine for the thorn, but the point of the fence is to keep stock in (or as it might be out of) a field. The cutting and laying of the thorns provides a living, organic hedge that just happens to be a highly effective form of stock proofing.

The one thing that I can tell you about hedge laying is that it is very difficult to do well. A hedge is usually laid after ten to fifteen years of growth. Hereunder is a very coarse guide as to how it is done.

All hedge laying is done during a period when the sap is not running (i.e. winter). Each stem is cut part way through with a nice clean cut as near the ground as possible. The stem is then bent over so that it is lying at an angle of roughly 30 degrees. The same thing is done with the next stem which lies on top of stem one and so on all the way down the fence. Every fifteen inches or so ('fist to elbow'), a vertical hazel stake is driven in – think of a woven hurdle.

The finished hedge should be straight up and down.

On one side, the growing brush wood will be left to keep the stock off the young growth. The other side of the fence, the side it was laid from, should be clean of growth. The trimmings will be piled up on the clean side as protection there.

To cap the job, a 'binder' of woven hazel wands is plaited along the top of the stakes to keep everything just where it should be and to add to the strength of the whole.

You will appreciate that the laid hedge is a living thing and starts growing again in the spring. In the first year, the new growth should achieve the thickness of a sixpenny piece.

At one time, the highly skilled art of hedge laying was nearly killed off by the growth of mechanical hedge-trimmers. I am glad to report that it has undergone a revival and is now alive and well. This revival has been partly due to the National Hedgecutting Society and partly due to the efforts of some hunts. Many of the hunts in the Midlands, where thorn fences flourish, have sponsored hedge laying for years and run annual competitions. For instance in 1930, in the Cottesmore Hunt country, thirty-one miles of laid fencing was judged: it took the judges nine days.

During the spring I was fortunate to able to attend the judging of the Cottesmore competition, which involved the inspection of over thirty different lengths of fencing in Rutland and Leicestershire. The work had been done by farmers and fencers through the winter.

Well and truly packed in a Land Rover the judges and our hosts bumped and thumped our way from hedge to hedge; across fields, down winding lanes and through quiet villages.

The laid lengths we looked at differed greatly. They had to be a minimum length of one chain (22 yards). The judges took immense trouble to inspect each entry in minute detail, judging the cut, the staking and the binder. The entries varied from downright scruffy, through 'a good tidy commercial job', to a length that even I could see was good; no, not just good, superb. It was beautifully laid, the cutting was as clean as can be, the staking was just so and the binder was as neat as a pig-tail.

'That,' said one of the judges, 'is a bit of whizzo.' I thought that that summed up the whole day: a day of glorious sunshine, in beautiful country, with good company. A day spent looking at examples of an age-old craft that has been revived. The good thing is that it has not been revived just as a gimmick but as something that is recognized as a form of fencing that is both commercially and environmentally sound: what a happy combination.

Chapter Fifty-Four

HUNTING WITH
THE JULY HOUNDS

I HAVE FOXHUNTED IN every month of the year except June. The circle has now been completed, but I had to go to Alabama to do it.

Benjamin H. Hardaway III, the Master of the Midland Hunt whom we met earlier in the book, hunts his hounds four days of the week during the winter; in the summer he just goes when he feels like it, maybe one or two days a week.

June in Alabama is hot. I do not mean English hot, I mean Hot Hot and Humid with it, the thermometer up in the 90s. This means that you have three hours after daybreak (at most) in which to hunt before the heat calls a halt.

It was still dark when we crossed the Chatteehoochee River into Alabama for a dawn meet at Cedar Heights. This part of Alabama is mostly scrub pine and brush. It was once prosperous with cotton until the bole weevil got to it; now there are large areas that are not good for much except foxhunting.

Hunting dress is not formal in the June heat. Braces and a cigar seem to be the form for the men. Stout boots and a pistol should also be worn, because this is rattlesnake country and we do not want any form of low life trying to mess with the Midland Hunt, do we?

Hounds came pouring out of the trailer. They are light-boned racy hounds, not unlike the English Fell hound. They are July hounds, one of the fourteen different breeds of foxhound to be found in America, and they are very much my type.

Butch, the local Game Warden, had been appointed to drive

the visitors in his pick-up and we were in radio contact with the hunt staff who all carry hand-sets on their saddles.

The Midland hounds hunt red fox, grey fox, bobcat and coyote with even handed conviction. 'The Swamp' seemed the favoured place to head for. Hounds and horses disappeared into the trees whilst David McGarr, a peanut farmer, and I took a turn down the dirt road. He pointed out the tracks of fox, bobcat and raccoon in the wet patches, but none of them was very fresh.

All was quiet except for the voice of the huntsman, some-where in the swamp. A high-pitched whimper; another, and then a swelling cry as more and more hounds joined in.

'They really pumpin' at him,' said David and then there he was on the track, a big grey fox looking at us. With a whisk of his brush he was back into the trees. 'Big old boar fox,' said Butch.

The Midland hounds do have marvellous voices.

'Hotdam, listen to that mouth,' said Benjamin H. as he came crashing out of the scrub and galloped away. I *was* listening and it made my back hairs stand up.

'Reckon he'll doodle around some now,' said David and I suppose that is a pretty fair description of how the Midland hounds flew for the next forty-five minutes and how we bumped and crashed and jolted our way through the Alabama woodlands in their wake.

Towards the end, the fox turned and headed back for the swamp. He came right past the pick-up. Everybody saw him except me: I was trying to get rid of some wretched chap on the radio who was wittering on about wheat straw and manure, neither of which interested me at that time.

A few minutes later hounds were marking at a large earth on the edge of the swamp. It was decided to give the fox best.

The heat was now becoming intense and it was time for home – but not before breakfast. Breakfast at the trailers was provided by the Upshaw and the Carroll families and how well Americans do these things. There was Brunswick Stew (watch out for the squirrel heads), barbecued pork ribs, potato salad, honey-cooked ham, fruit cake, pecan pie . . .

For perfect contentment, one of the trailers even had a 'Porta Potty'. Lawd ha' mercy; don't that beat all?

Chapter Fifty-Five

A GREAT PLACE
FOR THE THINKING

I HAVE BEEN KNOWN to brag about the view from my office window. Across the valley, the first green swelling off the Cheviot Hills fills the eye. Let the eye roam upwards and the blue shapes of higher and more distant hills can be seen. The view changes by the hour, sometimes by the minute, with contrasts of light and shade, whilst the base colours change with the seasons.

It is a seductive view. Sometimes I can resist it no longer. 'Bother Word Processors,' I say. 'Pish to Editors, subs and secretaries. Tush to telephones and fax machines. *I am off!*'

I lock the office door, put on my tackety boots, pick up my bait bag and my stick, and go.

There is a rough track that leads away from a certain bridge. It seems to have been thrown over the hill like a rope over a sack. It is the old track to a ruined steading far out in the hills and it seems as good a way to go as any.

It takes the first mile to get my wind and to get the bag settled into my back, then, as the slope eases off a bit, I manage to hit the stride, that long, slow, rolling-footed, slack-kneed stride that all men who habitually walk hills develop.

With every step the view changes minutely, the valley widens, a new valley opens up on the other hill, the horizon broadens as the path climbs higher and higher. Blackface sheep scatter momentarily as I pass, or merely watch my passing with their cynical horned faces.

The ruined steading sits in a little grove of stunted trees. It is a lonely but beautiful spot in a bowl of the hills. You would have to be dull of soul not to pause, lean on your stick and think for a moment of the generations of hardy people who lived and worked there. I tip my cap to their shades and set away onto the hill behind.

The hill is white with bog cotton. Larks climb above me. A curlew is whistling somewhere on the right and a raven croaks from the crags. Otherwise there is only the sound of the wind in the bent grass.

WHOOOSH! It is amazing how the jets can sneak up behind you and take you unaware. I am actually looking down on this chap. The scream blots out everything, then he is gone, hurdling the hill in front like a racehorse. That, I tell myself, was the 'sound of peace' and jolly good luck to them.

Here is an interesting thing. Someone has been cutting peat. There is a neat flap of turves racked up and set to dry in the sun and wind. At one time, this would have been the primary source of winter fuel for all the hill steadings, but very few people want to bother with such hard work now. What a wonderful smell peat smoke makes.

The climb becomes almost brutal. There is real heat in the sun now. The breathing is heavy and whilst I know that a man is only supposed to perspire, I have to tell you that I am sweating.

It is one of those maddening hills where you get to what you think must be the crest and there is another climb and another crest in front of you.

The actual top is not terribly exciting. It is a flat plateau of peat bog, a giant sponge which makes for poor walking. You have to weave and jump from tussock to heather patch – but what views. On one side the hills roll away to the distant Pennines. Men have told me that in certain weather conditions you can see the hills of the Lake District from here: even the most optimistic crow would reckon that distance as eighty miles.

As you walk round the plateau, the Scottish border is crossed. Far across the border lowlands is the blue line of what I assume to be the Lammermuirs. The wind is coming off the Irish Sea and brings with it the smell of miles of heather, peat moss and bracken. In spite of the warm sun, there is a distinct edge to the wind at 2000 plus feet.

Luncheon is taken under a sheltered rock. Ham sandwiches and a flask of tea and a view down the green eastern valleys to the blue of the distant sea. Then a pipe and the hat over the eyes as I listen to the silence.

Georgie was leaning on his stick by the bridge as I dropped back down the valley in the afternoon. 'Ye've been to the hill,' he said. 'It's a great place for the thinking.'

Chapter Fifty-Six

TO THE
DEFENCE OF
ROTTWEILERS

WE ARE A ROTTWEILER family. Jake was twelve weeks old when he first came to us. He grew into eight stone of bone, muscle, power and intelligence. I have handled a great number of dogs during my life and he was certainly one of the cleverest.

He was a dog of very great charm and character. The phrase 'Gentle Giant' has become something of a cliché, but it summed up our big black dog absolutely. Mind you, if a stranger had taken it into his head to attempt to slip unobtrusively into our house at one o'clock in the morning (as it might be to borrow a cup of sugar) then I do not think that things would have gone well for the visitor. Jake had strong views about the sanctity of the family patch.

I am much saddened by the bad things that have been happening to Rottweilers recently. The Collie Dog men have a saying that 'there are no bad dogs; only bad handlers'. This is a slight over-simplification, but is mostly true.

Rottweilers have always been loyal servants and friends to Man. They are of very ancient lineage. The Romans used their forebears as guard dogs. Middle European drovers used them to drove and guard cattle. On the successful conclusion of their business, it was the drovers' custom to put their guilders in a purse tied round a Rottweiler neck; they could then make whoopee in the Gräf und Fraulein, knowing that their savings were secure.

In more recent times, Rottweilers have been used by various police forces. The Austrian Army Dog Section is entirely dogged with Rottweilers.

Right then, so what you have is a very large and powerful dog that has been bred for a very long time to guard and protect its own social unit to which it forms a fierce loyalty: all very right and proper. Now they have become victims of human failings: greed, fashion and false pride.

The troubles began when the Rottweiler became fashionable. This is the worst disaster that can overtake any breed of dog. I am given to understand that over recent years the Rottweiler population in this country has increased tenfold. With puppies commanding £300 a time, many unscrupulous breeders have come crawling out of the woodwork and have bred from stock that was both physically and temperamentally substandard.

These substandard dogs have been bought by substandard owners. They have been bought as status symbols by people who know nothing about dogs in general, or Rottweilers in particular. These people do not have the resources, skill or knowledge to cope with their acquisition. Such a combination is a disaster looking for somewhere to happen.

You can live in ignorance and mutual incomprehension with a Yorkshire terrier and the result will probably be no more than mild irritation amongst your neighbours: ten stone of frustrated, soured Rottweiler can be dangerous.

So, what is to be done? I am glad to say that some positive steps are being taken. The other day I accompanied Graham Mabbutt (dog handler extraordinary) to a meeting of the North-East Rottweiler Obedience Club. Graham was to do character assessments with Dr Malcolm Willis, Senior Lecturer in Genetics at Newcastle University.

John Richardson, the Club Chairman, explained that the Club was formed by a group of dedicated Rottweiler owners to improve the training of both dogs *and owners*. The members very properly believe that the Rottweiler is a specialist dog and requires specialist handling. The club is very much a family affair with the emphasis on the dogs being integrated into the family, which is as it should be.

The club never turns away a dog and owner, no matter how difficult a problem they seem to present. Colin Lawrence, the Club Trainer, did admit that there were occasions when the relationship between a particular dog and its owner were beyond repair. The happy human and canine atmosphere of the club was impressive and such initiatives can only be good for the future of the Rottweiler. Anything that can save these splendid and intelligent dogs from becoming victims of ignorance, greed and misinformation must be good.

Our much loved Jake dropped dead the other day. His death caused us much grief. By the time you read this there will be another Rottweiler taking up too much space in front of the Rayburn. There will never be another Jake, but the house would not be home without a Rottweiler.

The Romans used their fore bears as guard dogs

Chapter Fifty-Seven

WHEN AUTUMN IS IN THE AIR

I LIKE THE AUTUMN. It comes hard, clean and sharp after the soggy, sweaty, dog-end days of late summer. There comes a day when the early morning air has a definite bite to it. The wind from the hill makes you shiver in your shirtsleeves, but brings with it the scents of heather and bracken that make you wiggle your nose. Autumn is in the air and it puts a skip into the step. This is just as well because there is a lot to be done in the autumnal countryside; in fact, it is probably the busiest time of year for many people. So many things happen at once, or overlap.

There is the harvest to finish. There then is the straw to bale and lead (carry). As soon as the field is clear, it is ready to plough, disc, harrow and then drill with winter corn. There are no 'hours' to this sort of work. The work continues as long as the weather permits. Many times this autumn I have looked out of my window at night and seen the lights of tractors working into the little hours.

I do not grow corn so I can get to bed of nights. This is just as well because, for me, the autumn is a time of early mornings.

I like the early mornings; as my old friend Tommy says, 'You cannot beat a good start in the morning.' There is a lot to be done on a sheep farm in the autumn. Sheep are prone to succumb to all sorts of strange diseases: how would you fancy Grothels, Gid, Husk or Orf? Perhaps you would prefer a quick burst of Braxy, Blackleg or Kebbing? Take it from me that you would not want any of them — and we do not want our sheep to get them, either. In the autumn, the flockmaster carries a multi-shot injector strapped to one thigh. On the other thigh is an automatic dosing gun with which to zap the wily Nematode and discomfort the fatal Liver Fluke.

The battle also continues on the outside of the sheep, where lurk the Blowfly and the Scabmite. These are dealt with by dipping. The sheep are made to enter a tub full of a nasty chemical cocktail where they have to swim for about for a minute while a man dunks them with a dipping crook. Dipping is good for sheep but, like humans, sheep hate being done good to. This makes it hard work. I once dipped two thousand sheep in one day, and that is why I have large arms.

Autumn is the time of the sheep sales (our harvest). There are ewe sales, lamb sales and tup (ram) sales. Hundreds of thousands of sheep and millions of pounds go through these sales. The livelihood of a multitude of farmers depend on them, so they stimulate the adrenalin somewhat. For all that, they also provide a chance to meet old friends and if we should have a nip together for old times' sake, who would deny us that pleasure.

The autumn is lobster time. My friends Bill and Ray Stanton make their living from the sea and sometimes they take me with them. Sometimes I wish that they had not. Everyday they lift, empty, re-bait (bits of dead mackerel – are you sorry you asked?) and return to the deep 240 pots. The North Sea is not always a friendly place. The next time you guzzle a lobster, spare a thought for the men who get them for you and who live 'in the hands of God and nature'.

The swallows who nested in my sheep shed and garage have reared their broods and gone. Soon the first skeins of southward-flying geese will appear. The autumn is also the time for the grouse and the partridge. I do not shoot myself, but I can understand the excitement when a great pack of grouse lifts out of the heather. It seems to have been a good year for the partridge. There is a covey that lives part-time on my farm. They are jolly little birds and I like to see them about.

I am also hoping to see lots of duck this winter. George has dug me a spendid duck pond at the bottom of the farm, in spite of his bulldozer sinking to the tops of the tracks at one time. I hope some of the duck will choose to breed on the island, but I will have to do something about the mink in the burn before nesting time.

The clatter of hooves down the lane increases. People are getting their hunters fit for the coming season. It takes two months of long slow work to get a horse basically fit. I shall never again feel the surging thrill of a galloping horse, but I have my shepherding boots and my horn heid stick. I can still watch the graceful beauty of the fox slipping through the bracken. I can still see hounds on a distant hillside, swooping and driving like a flock of white birds. The excitement of their wild, fierce voices carried on the wind can still force me into an undignified jog for a better vantage point; then my knee cracks and reminds me that I, too, am coming into autumn.

Chapter Fifty-Eight

THE
WESER VALE HUNT

THERE IS NO PROPER hunting in Germany. Hitler stopped it because he thought it was cruel. Post-war German governments have continued to respect his preference for guns and gas. This may tell you a lot about the Germans.

The British Army of Occupation took packs of foxhounds with them as a matter of course. Foxhunting stopped with the restoration of German sovereignty. The ever resourceful Brits simply turned their attention to hunting men. This form of hunting is known as the 'Clean Boot', which means that hounds hunt only the scent of the man with no artificial additives. The best hounds for this job are bloodhounds, or bloodhounds X foxhounds.

The only remaining pack of 'Boot Hounds' is the Weser Vale and they celebrated their twentieth anniversary in 1989. They were founded, and are still maintained, by the Household Cavalry, one regiment of which is always in Germany. I attended a recent meet at the Officers' Mess of the Blues and Royals, near Senelager. The Blues and Royals seek excellence in everything and their hospitality is no exception to this admirable rule.

The scene at the meet was no different from a meet of foxhounds in England, except that the quarry (Lt Andrew Wilkinson) was also at the meet, flexing his muscles and tightening his sinews with an invigorating glass of port. He then loped off into the wide yonder of the Senelager training range. After ten minutes 'law' and perhaps another glass of port, Lt William Wakeham (the huntsman) moved off with his six couple of hounds to hunt down his ferocious prey.

There was a field of about twenty under the stern eye of Major Toby Browne. All ranks and several regiments were represented, as well as a few German civilians. I was driven with great cavalry élan by Capt Gerry McCullough.

We hurried to a bridge across a seething main road. Quarry, hounds and full supporting cast were confidently expected to cross the bridge, but such is the speed of events with the Weser Vale that we could do no more than look sadly at recent hoof prints.

There were two hunts scheduled for the day. Four is the norm, but the area available was somewhat restricted by the military activities of the Bundeswehr (German Army). We took up a position for the second line in the hope that this time we should see the 'full panoply of the chase unfold'.

The waiting time was helped by the arrival of Mrs Gordon Birdwood with a carload of goodies, something which seldom happens during the rather more rugged sport of foxhunting. So we munched and sipped and raised our glasses to the sweating figure of Lt Wilkinson as he burst out of the undergrowth.

'The b——s killed me the last time,' he said as he thundered past. I must say he looked very well on it.

The booming cry of the hounds got louder and I climbed a bank to get a view. The big black hounds came surging across the open heath and stopped to eye me speculatively: a potential meal? I was very properly rebuked by the huntsman for distracting his hounds. They then harooshed and boomed away and we were able to cast a critical eye over the mounted followers as they made the most of the jumps which are scattered about the heath.

The Quarry had obligingly doubled back so we were able to stay with Mrs Birdwood's hospitality and watch the final stage of the hunt which ended in Lt Wilkinson covered in muddy pad marks and with a severely licked face.

It was then time for a tour of the stables and riding school. This amazing complex was built without one penny of public money being used. It allows all-weather equitation to take place and is used for training men and horses for mounted duties when the regiment returns to England.

Hounds are snugly kennelled in some converted pigsties. They are lovingly cared for on a voluntary basis by Trooper Gladstone, a truly happy man. The maintenance of the kennels is looked after by a German supporter: Herr Hundescheidt (no jest, I assure you).

The German civilian financial support is vital to the hunt. It is interesting to note that the Anglo-German Community Relations Fund subscribes to the hunt because of the goodwill that it produces, most especially amongst the farming community.

The members of the Weser Vale Hunt are some of the best ambassadors the British Army has amongst the German people. They have a lot of fun as well.

Chapter Fifty-Nine

WAR GAMES

In 1794, the British Government introduced a bill for 'encouraging and disciplining such corps and companies of men, as shall voluntarily enrol themselves for the Defence of their counties, towns or coasts, or for the General Defence of the Kingdom, during the present war'. The mounted arm of these volunteers were known as 'Gentlemen and Yeomanry Cavalry'. The men provided their own horses; saddlery and uniforms were paid for by the officers of the units. It followed from this that the officers tended to be men of wealth and property and the ranks were mainly filled with small freeholders and tenant farmers: the Yeomanry.

In the first half of the nineteenth century, the Yeomanry were mainly used for what would now be known as 'internal security' duties. The spirit of revolution was abroad in Europe and the years to 1850 were spattered with riots and agrarian unrest. In the absence of any proper police force, the Yeomanry became the main 'aid to the civil power', which was counted unto them as righteousness in some quarters, but not in others.

Yeomanry units first saw action overseas during the South African War and subsequently served with distinction during the Kaiser's War. Many Yeomanry regiments were still horsed at the beginning of the Hitler War. They were all eventually mechanized but not before units of the 5th Cavalry Brigade (North Somerset Yeomanry, Yorkshire Dragoons and Cheshire Yeomanry) mounted the British Army's last cavalry charge; it was against the Vichy French in Syria.

The Yeomanry regiments have suffered many ups and downs since the last war, but like all true cavalrymen they have picked themselves up, dusted themselves off and re-mounted. Today, they are the cavalry arm of the Territorial Army.

The Queen's Own Yeomanry (QOY) is the result of amalgamation in 1971 of the Queen's Own Yorkshire Yeomanry, the Northumberland Hussars, the Cheshire Yeomanry and the Ayrshire Yeomanry. It is probably fair to say that the QOY has maintained its rural roots more than most. The reason that a fox was chosen for the cap badge of the new regiment was that four of the five Honorary Colonels at the time of amalgamation were Masters of Foxhounds.

The role of the QOY is that of a TA armoured reconnaissance regiment which makes them part of the British Army of the Rhine. This means that should the Russian Bear get stroppy, the merry men of the QOY are out of their civilian suits, into their armoured cars and off to Germany like long dogs. To fight in Germany, they must on occasion pry enough money out of the politicians to go and exercise there. This they did during the autumn of 1989, taking with them a Heavily Unarmed Civilian Scribe (HUCS) with his combat notebook, sleeping bag and his knifeforkspoonmug; those inseparable companions of life in the field.

I suppose that I had better put you in the picture on the military situation.

The North German plain was about to be invaded by Orange Force, representing those who would once more plunge Europe into the reeking abyss of savagery. This part was taken by the Belgians, represented by the 4th Chasseurs à Cheval, and the Panzeraufklarungs Batt 1 from our NATO German allies (known to the British Army as the Bundeskrauts). The forces of civilisation ranged against these monsters were the 16th/5th Lancers and the Queen's Dragoon Guards (regular) and the QOY and the Royal Yeomanry: all reconnaissance regiments with light armoured vehicles. It was to be a confrontation of free and fast-flowing action.

Regimental Headquarters (QOY) had made itself very comfortable in a huge German barn. German farmers are very keen on growing armoured cars in their barns. They get 'Barn Money'.

A derelict cottage hid the Officers Mess. Attached to it by a camouflage net was that most vital of all military vehicles – Zero Hotel – the mess truck. From the cramped deeps of Zero Hotel, the justly famous Staff Sergeant Knott (a restaurant manager back in the world) seemed to be able to produce hot meals at any given moment. He was to be put to a stern test that night for the officers were to dine their Honorary Colonel, the redoubtable Sir Ralph Carr-Ellison, MFH, in a final gastronomic flurry before the war started.

I have to say that the QOY do their guests jolly well. There was champagne and claret and port. Excellent veal steaks and compo cheese; my bit of compo cheese had a large black thumb mark on it, but David Cave-Biggley (aka Biggles), the medical officer and distinguished Cheshire surgeon, assured me that thumb prints were good for the libido, or was it the cheese? My notes get a bit blurred at this point. The conversation was on an appropriately high plane, although the mess may have been aghast at the insults traded between the Scribe and the Hon Colonel. They were not to know that insults are our normal conversational currency.

And so to bed: sleeping bags on the hard floorboards with the North German wind whistling through a cracked window pane: my last taste of luxury for a bit.

Ablutions under a cold tap make a chap ready for breakfast, but nothing prepared me for the baroque horrors of the Prussian thunderbox that lurked in a corner of the barn. Clegged to the wall outside the door was a sign with the slogan: 'Alles Frisch' which I think advertised apples. It certainly did not give a true and fair description of the thunderbox.

The situation was deteriorating. Orange Force was deemed to have made a seaborne landing and their forces were even then advancing across the peaceful German countryside.

It was time to get the 'Train Set' (as the QOY call their regiment) in action. I suppose it is inevitable that if you have a train set, then the man in charge must be known as 'The Fat

Controller': this is a gross slander on the dapper figure of Lt Col Nick Tuck (Royal Hussars) who was commanding the regiment for the last time before becoming Military Attaché in Kuala Lumpur. All TA units have a stiffening of regular training and admin staff.

I was handed over to the Training Major, Major Johnny Shaw, a Beau Sabreur of the Blue and Royals, and his driver, the imperturbable and ever resourceful Trooper Stokoe. We were off to the war.

As a reconnaissance regiment, the QOY is highly mobile. The squadrons and their component troops are scattered about the countryside — watching and waiting; their role is to observe without being seen themselves.

We stumbled across Y Squadron cunningly disguised as a coniferous plantation. Y is the Yorkshire Squadron.

Second Lt Hugo Willis is a student at York University. He was kind enough to let me inspect his Fox armoured car. It took two men to lever me into the commander's seat and three to get me out. A Fox may have a 4.2 litre Jaguar engine, but I am here to tell you that it is uncomfortable and, I would think, extremely drafty. I was not mad about the colour scheme either. I suggested to Y Squadron that were I to go to war then I would join the Foot Guards. Y Squadron seem to think that it would recover from the disappointment.

We set off once more on our travels. Travel in the back of a military Land Rover can best be described as character building. The back of the Land Rover also contained the bedding, the rations, the stove, the water and the lovely Ms Arron, photo-graphiste extraordinary: we were indeed a huddled mass.

The Trainer was doing the navigating in the front. Cavalry Navigation seems to require a sort of ritual incantation. It goes something like this: 'Oh-shit-wrong-road-turn-round-Stokoe-sorry-about-that-everyone.' I imagine that it is taught at Sandhurst.

RHQ had relocated itself and took a bit of finding, which is the idea after all — can't have RHQ being 'bounced' by the enemy, now can we? It hardly needs saying that RHQ had found itself a nice barn. The barn belonged to Otto — huge, black-bearded and smiling. Otto took a great personal interest in the progress of the war as did Mrs Otto, Otto's father and mother, all the many little Ottos and the resident Rottweiler and Alsatian dogs.

Dinners were now less formal affairs. The Brigadier commanding the exercise had declared it officially 'dry': he was not a cavalryman. There was a certain wistful remembrance of the fact that the Northumberland Hussars had driven off to Hitler's War with a three-tonner laden with Kümmel – the revolting gripe water so loved by the Northumbrian Gentry. Of course anyone who felt off-colour was perfectly entitled to apply to the doctor for something medicinal and restorative.

After dinner I talked to Major John Dalrymple Hamilton, then the Second-in-Command of the regiment and Commanding Officer Designate. He had joined the Ayrshire Squadron of the QOY straight from university. He was then working for Scottish and Newcastle Breweries, and he now farms in Ayrshire. A quiet man, his dedication and commitment to the QOY is obvious. He admits that his farming suffers at times. He says that he is fortunate that his family accept that he spends one weekend in two soldiering, but they do not like it. Family pressures cause a lot of men to give up the TA.

'Tommy the Tent tonight,' said the Trainer. Question: how many soldiers, plus a Lady Photographer and a Jumbo Journo, can you fit in a small bivouac tent? The answer is: three, more or less.

With the grey German dawn comes cold water ablutions, shovel patrol (do not ask) and breakfast of compo sausage sandwiches, lashings of tea and a keen discussion on theology with the Padre, the Rev Toddy Hoare: there can be no finer way to start a day.

'Today we find the war,' said the Trainer and I must say it had been notable for its absence so far. We thought that we must find it on the Küsten Kanal, which the invaders had to cross.

On the banks of the canal I talked to members of the A Squadron Support Troop who were guarding a bridge. Corporal McMurdo was unemployed, and had been eight years in the regiment. Trooper Jardine was a builder's labourer and

Trooper Maclaren an electrician. They were all obviously devoted to the QOY and all thoroughly enjoyed it. By now it had become clear to me that the Territorial Army is not just a part-time interest for its members, it is a way of life and one that is not always easy to fit in with domestic commitments: the plaintive phrase 'women just don't seem to understand' could almost be a TA motto.

The war was not going well for the planners. The enemy should have forced the canal by now. In fact, the Queens Dragoon Guards had put up such a spirited defence that the enemy was still ten K (kilometres) away and going backwards.

'Germans got no balls,' said a laconic Carl Gustav anti-tank weapon by the bridge.

Balls or not, Orange Forces got moving that night by the simple expedient of crossing the canal by all the bridges that had been demolished on paper, if not in fact. Cheating it might be but it did get things moving.

It was unfortunate that the 'flap' developed during dinner. Zero Hotel had switched to combat mode at the start of hostilities, and the regiment now lived on compo rations. The Trainer (canny fellow) had laid in tinned supplies of 'Cassoulet de Cardenac au Porc' and 'Cassoulet au Confit de Canard'. Trooper Stokoe was just bringing this to mouth-watering perfection on his spirit stove, when the Trainer was urgently summoned to RHQ. I thought that he had been pushing his luck. As Training Major, he officially had only a watching brief and was not directly involved in the beastliness. In the name of Press Relations, it had become our pleasant custom to leave the war to its own devices each day, whilst we sought a leisurely luncheon in a local hostelry. Descriptions of these lunches to a highly-strung Colonel confined to compo rations and tinned stew, had brought a steely gleam to that gentleman's eye. The axe now fell. The trainer was no longer a by-stander.

I thought that I had better let him know that the cassoulet had been quite excellent, so, having wiped my moustache, I too sought out RHQ. The tiny cramped space was full of crackling wireless traffic, furiously scribbling officers, half-eaten plates of stew, and tension. I cannot think that the tension was being eased by Otto, still smiling and leaning hugely on the central tent post, whilst two little Ottos, the Alsatian and the Rotteweiler chased each other in and out of everybody's feet. At this moment there came a message from Exercise HQ that the defenders were to assume that ninety-five Russian tanks had broken through on the eastern flank and that they had better get their backsides out and quick. The point being that everybody had to be in an allocated area on the Dutch border by Friday night because heavy vehicles (like armoured cars) are not allowed on German roads over the weekend. I do hope that the Soviet General Staff is cognizant of this fact. I thought that it was my bedtime. It had begun to rain.

All through the night, as I dozed somewhat fitfully, I could hear the whine of hard-driven armoured cars as the pull-back continued. I thought of the men, wet, cold and tired in their armoured cars. I thought of the red-eyed, sleepless tension in RHQ ('Switch to high power and work through it'). I asked myself whether I would thus give up six weeks of my spare time every year. The short answer is no, but I can see why men become fervent members of the QOY. The regiment has spirit, style and tradition. It gives men a pride, a purpose and a meaning which civilian life does not always supply. Like all good regiments it is also a family, and a proud and happy one at that.

Chapter Sixty

DE RIGUEUR

NOVEMBER BRINGS THE official start of the foxhunting season. With the season proper, out comes the proper kit, the real gear, the formal uniform of the hunting field.

Hunting has been going on for some time before November, of course. 'Autumn Hunting' starts as soon as the state of the harvest permits. In wilder parts of the country, where corn comes only in bottled form, hunting may well have started early in August.

This pre-season hunting is not very formal. Hounds tend to meet at daybreak and very few people attend. Those who do, come in all shapes and conditions of dress. Nobody minds.

After the Opening Meet, however, people do mind. To be scruffily turned out is bad manners and is an insult to those whose land you are going to ride over. This is not to say that everything worn has to be new; it just has to be clean and tidy. That is surely not too much to ask.

What does the well-dressed hunting person wear? Let us start at the top and work down.

A person only has one head and it pays to protect it. The velvet hunting cap is now worn by most people in the hunting field. It is, in fact, a crash helmet. A properly fitted cap should stay on your head whilst you fall on it. Badly fitting caps do not and people keep them on with complicated chin strap harnesses. These have the added advantage (if properly adjusted) of stopping wearers talking too much: for which relief, much thanks. Black hunting caps are only worn by Hunt Officials and Farmers. The Punters wear caps of many funny colours. The Top Hat is an endangered species as are the people who still wear them.

Around the neck goes a 'stock tie'. This is a complicated scarf arrangement that looks good if it is tied properly, but too often looks like a pudding cloth. It should be *tight*. A properly tied stock tie will support the neck when falling. The ration is one neck per person. The normal colour for stock ties these days is white. Old Toffs in top hats might wear a blue bird's-eye stock tie.

The coat: black coats are the most numerous. They are easy to clean. Regular (and paying) followers of a hunt may be given the hunt button (every hunt has its own design). This is the equivalent of getting your House Colours, and only the Master can award it. Once buttoned, the follower can either stay black or can set up in a *red* coat: never, never, never pink. Hunt coats are always 'body coats': this is the tailors' technical name for the way they are cut. A good coat will last a long time. It is worthwhile going to a good hunting tailor and having a coat properly built. Let it be made of thick hard cloth and let it be lined and lined again; then, even when it is sodden, it will keep the body warm.

Next come the breeches. There are few more intimate relationships than that which exists between a person and his or her breeches. There is a great vogue for stretch nylon breeches at the moment: they are easy to fit and will machine-wash. I am prepared to admit that the contour-clinging qualities of stretch breeches has added a new, and often delightful, dimension to the female members of the hunting field.

Men in stretch breeches definitely lack glamour. Thin men look like scarecrows; fat men bulge in a most unseemly manner. Apart from that, nylon breeches are thin, cold and nasty. Stick to cavalry twill or Bedford cord and, for real comfort, have them cut like the breeches of our old friend in the top hat: plenty of room in the base area.

Rubber boots are comparatively cheap, but they are cold, clammy and give no protection against a kick. Leather boots are teeth-grindingly expensive but will last for years if they are looked after properly. That means 'boning': working the leather with the leg bone of a red deer (after the deer has finished with it). I am probably the only person left in Britain who knows how to bone boots.

Black boots with a black coat. Black boots with brown tops with a red coat. A garter strap should always be worn between the boot and the knee. It no longer has any practical purpose, but a boot looks wrong without it.

Modern spurs do not have much practical purpose either, but again the boot looks naked without them. The buckle goes on the outside of the boot. The neck of the spur should point down and not up. A person who puts their spurs on upside down is likely to trip over them coming out of the pub and fall on his head – which brings us neatly back to where we started.

Chapter Sixty-One

FOXHUNTING
IN THE NINETIES

A T THE BEGINNING OF November, Foxhound packs in Great Britain will be celebrating the official start of the hunting season. The scene has changed little in the last hundred years. The centre of attention will be the huntsman and the hounds, a shifting mass of lemon, white and tan, with lolling tongues and waving sterns. To the huntsman, the hounds are his children. He knows them all as individuals: their strengths and their weaknesses and he loves them dearly.

The Hunt Staff (Huntsman and his assistant, the Whipper-in) are in their best uniforms: black hunting cap, white stock tie, red coat, brilliant white breeches and mirror-polished boots.

The followers too will all be dressed in their very best; turned out, we hope, as advised in the previous chapter. Horses will be gleaming and probably over-fresh, which will not always go well with their riders' opening meet nerves.

At the opening meet, there will be people from all walks of life. They are all there for one reason: they love foxhunting and the opening meet is one of the great occasions on their calendar.

What is the state of foxhunting in Britain at the start of a new decade.

There are 194 packs of foxhounds in England and Wales. These packs total some 21,400 days' hunting every season. There are reckoned to be 48,000 mounted followers and some 400,000 people who follow regularly by car, bicycle, or on foot. In addition to this, it is estimated that one million people attend at least one hunt during the season. For instance, the police estimate that 5000 people attend the Boxing Day meet of the Quorn in Loughborough Market Place.

Foxhunting has always attracted a wide cross-section of society. There are several hunting Dukes (Marlborough, Beaufort and more).

Ian Coe is not a duke, he drives a tractor and is a desperate keen hunting man. It is difficult to think of any section of society that does not have a representative in the hunting field. Foxhunting is obviously a rural sport and the countryside has traditionally provided the bulk of its support, but many of the people who are taking up hunting today come from the towns.

Hunting is an expensive operation and the introduction of new income has been welcome, but the increase of numbers has also brought problems. Many people do not realize that nearly all hunting takes place on private land and it *only* happens with the consent of the landowners; the vast majority of farmers in England and Wales allow hunting over their land. Those who do stop the hunt tend to do so for purely practical reasons.

Farmers today are under great pressure; from the politicians, the public, the banks. They are worried men; do they need the hunt as well? More especially, do they need a lot of people they do not know and who have little knowledge of farming or country life galloping across their farm?

Brian Wood has a large beef, sheep and arable farm in Northumberland. He does not hunt himself. He does not think that the hunt has very much effect on his farming generally, as long as they keep off any newly-sown grass leys and keep away at peak calving times. He feels very strongly that people who hunt should understand farming and what is happening in the countryside. He feels that 'uncontrolled townies' would be a major problem. It seems that some New Hunters think that they have a divine right to cross land. This attitude is not acceptable to farmers.

To be fair, this attitude is not acceptable either to the hunts who are mindful of this problem. The Holderness Hunt in East Yorkshire, who draw many urban supporters from Hull and its environs, hold seminars for their New Hunters to explain the ways of hunting and the countryside.

David Obsorne was one of the founders of these 'teach-ins'. The formula is very simple. The Hunt takes a room in a hotel and invites any members who they think might be interested. There is a panel of experienced hunting people, and great efforts are made to bring in people with acknowledged expertise; the panel always includes the professional huntsman. All aspects of hunting are discussed in a question-and-answer session: dress, manners, customs, hounds, kennel management, the handling of hounds out hunting, horn calls, hunting language and the importance of discipline. In other words, 'all the things that people who have been brought up with hunting take for granted, but which can seem totally obscure and strange to those who have recently taken up the sport'. Drinks and eats are provided and the aim is to have a good social evening as well as an informative one. These teach-ins are held every hunting season, but there are plans to hold them even more frequently.

Many hunts limit 'hooves on the ground'.

Some years ago, the Quorn Hunt was getting fields of over two hundred horses on certain days. It was too many. The hunt canvassed opinion amongst the farmers and Major Charles Humfrey, the Hunt Secretary, drew up a scheme to limit numbers. Subscribers now have to nominate the day of the week on which they wish to hunt and they are then only allowed to hunt on that particular day. So if a person on the Monday list wishes to hunt on a Friday, he has to ask to be put on the Friday list as well and pay another subscription. Every year, there are some twenty people on the waiting list to join the Quorn.

Capt Ian Farquhar is Joint Master with the Duke of Beaufort. The Beaufort have no waiting list, they simply do not allow anyone from outside their hunting country to become members. However, they do have a lot of New Hunters. Capt Farquhar thinks that the biggest class of New Hunters are the children of working people. These people are not particularly wealthy, but have done well enough in recent years to be able to keep a pony for their children. These children are now coming out hunting. As much as seventy percent of the Beaufort field (c.150 on a Saturday) is still made up of farmers and their families.

One of the problems of foxhunting is that it does require a great deal of space in which to operate. Space is becoming a scarce commodity in modern England: every year more countryside is gobbled up by building development and new roads; every year the space available for hunting shrinks.

Even in rural Dorset the pressure is being felt. Ted Lycett-Green, the Master of the Portman, talks of tumbledown buildings once covered with brambles and where he would have drawn for a fox. These buildings are now being done up by yuppies who have 'double-glazed lawns'. The trouble is that the Portman foxes do not understand about double glazing.

There is no doubt that many hunts are going to have to amalgamate or disappear. The North Warwickshire disbanded after their hunting country became unviable through building and motorways. Milton Keynes forced the amalgamation of the Whaddon Chase and Bicester Hunts. The Channel Tunnel is certainly going to force a redrawing of the hunting map in the south-eastern corner of England.

Then there are Politics and the Media. It has to be said that most politicians and journalists know nothing about hunting. To be fair to them, they received very little positive information about hunting until fairly recently. The information they did receive tended to be the propaganda of the various anti-hunting factions for whom hunting is mainly a battle in the Class War. For many years the attitude of hunting people to their bad press was to ignore it and hope that it would go away. Now the Masters of Foxhounds Association and Brian Toon, their Public Relations Officer, have adopted a more robust approach to what they regard as mischievous misinformation. The result of this new attitude is that various hunts have thirty-one Actions for Defamation currently in progress: four have already been won this year and Mr Toon says that they have not lost one yet.

There are those who say that hunting in Britain will not

survive the next Labour Government and/or the Channel Tunnel. They said the same about the canals, the railways, the Kaiser and Hitler.

Hunting is with us yet.

What are the top packs of foxhounds in 1990? Who hunts in Division One? Hereunder is a highly personal and maybe somewhat eccentric selection.

Duke of Beaufort's – Gloucestershire/Avon: Reached the height of its fame under the late Duke who was universally known as 'Master'. The present Duke presides with great flair. Hounds are hunted by Capt Ian Farquhar who has charm, style, looks and is also a fine huntsman. It is enough to make you spit with envy. As already mentioned, you have to live in the Beaufort country to be allowed to hunt there, so do not get too over excited.

Border – Northumberland: The wild border hills and the wild border foxes might not be to everyone's taste. The people are wilder yet. However, these are some of the best foxcatching hounds in the realm. The mastership is a father and son team: Ian and Michael Hedley. Michael is a laidback genius of a huntsman who looks like Woody Allen. Not a country for faint hearts, lack of stamina, or teetotallers.

Cheshire – Cheshire. None of the current mastership is known to me, but I do know the professional huntsman, Johnny O'Shea. He has shown great sport in this lovely grass country since 1966. He is one of the best professional huntsmen and amateur humorists in the country.

Cotley – Devon: This delightful pack of West Country harriers (a breed of hound) has been in the Eames family since the eighteenth century. The late Col Dick Eames was a superb huntsman and one of my great heroes.

Cotswold – Gloucestershire: Perhaps my favourite amongst the Gloucestershire hunting countries. Presided over by genial giant Tim Unwin, whom an American lady described as being 'straight out of Central Casting'. Be that as it may, he is a fine hunstman and an astute breeder of hounds.

Devon and Somerset Staghounds: Staghunting gets a lot of stick in the media, but you should make up your own minds. The people of Exmoor have no doubts. Everything stops when the staghounds are about and little else is talked about in the pubs at night. Denis Boyles has hunted the D&S since 1971. I wish I could get down there more often.

Dumfriesshire: This pack of huge, black-and-tan hounds and their Master (Sir Rupert Buchanan-Jardine, Bt) are unique and very definitely in my personal Top Ten.

Exmoor: Capt R. E. Wallace is probably the greatest fox-hunter of our time. That really says it all.

The Fell Packs – **Melbreak, Blencathra, Ullswater, Eskdale and Ennerdale, Coniston, North Lonsdale, Lunesdale**: I have lumped these together because they are all excellent. They hunt the rugged Lakeland fells and are followed on foot. This is foxhunting with no frills attached; unless you include tattypot suppers and singing.

Leicestershire: Not so very long ago, the English Midlands were a sea of old pasture which was famous for the feeding of bullocks. By virtue of that fact, the grass fields were strongly fenced. This combination made Leicestershire a very happy hunting ground. Melton Mowbray became the most famous and fashionable hunting centre in the world. The three hunts that converged on Melton also became famous and fashionable: they are the **Belvoir** (Beaver), the **Cottesmore** and the **Quorn**. They remain famous and fashionable: they still have pockets of old grass and wire-free fences, but they also have funny habits like stopping for lunch in the middle of a day's hunting (yes, I know they say they are stopping to change horses, but I know that that should take thirty seconds, not half an hour). There is now much better hunting to be had in other parts of Great Britain. However, Leicestershire remains socially gilt-edged and I understand that the '*aprés chasse*' is irreproachable.

Tynedale – also Northumberland: Some people consider this to be the best all-round foxhunting country left in England. The Hunt went through a pretty sticky period but has been rescued by a triumulierate of the most beautiful and formidable lady masters in England (which is saying quite a lot). The Tynedale foxes and hounds now go like the wind and so would I in their place.

West Percy – Northumberland: A lovely wild hill country and one of the best packs of hounds in the country. George

Trotter is the professional huntsman. I am one of the Joint Masters. What more could anyone ask?

Wilts, South and West: I have to mention the SWW because my brother-in-law is Master and it is still one of the nicest countries in the south. Captain Simon Clarke (the in-law) was one of the best huntsmen in the realm and is also one of the sharpest minds in foxhunting. Like me, he has had to give up carrying the horn due to the increasing weight of his responsibilities.

Every year the space available to hunting shrinks

Chapter Sixty-Two

A FAMILY OF MAIDENS

ALL COUNTRY PEOPLE recognize the importance of breeding and heredity. They know that 'blood will out' and that the study of blood lines is something that you ignore at your peril. This truth applies just as much to the human animal as it does to the four-legged kind, however unpalatable this fact may be to social engineers. There are certain people who should never be bred from.

Selective breeding has always played a part in preserving the stability and cohesion of rural society. Thus you not only get the same people owning the same land for many years, but you also get the same families farming and working on the same estates, or following the same craft or profession for generation after generation.

To demonstrate this point, let us ignore the 10th Duke of This, or the 14th Viscount That (although they are both charming fellows) and let us consider my friend Jack Maiden and his family.

Jack was born in 1920 and spent his whole working life in the service of the foxhound. As a boy, he worked with his father who was then First Whipper-in and Kennel Huntsman at the Whaddon Chase Hunt. It is normal practice in Hunt Service for men to move about as they progress up the ladder. Jack served, at various times, with the North Hertfordshire, South Dorset, North Cotswold, Middleton East, Fitzwilliam, Pytchley, Braes of Derwent, West Percy and finally as Huntsman to the Minehead.

What sets a man off on a way of life that is uncertain,

sometimes dangerous and always physically and mentally demanding? I do not suppose that Jack ever considered any other way of life: hunting was in his blood.

In about 1720, one Joe Maiden was Huntsman to a Mr Forrester whose hounds hunted in East Shropshire in what is now the Wheatland Hunt country. It seems certain that his son Will eventually succeed him in the same post.

Not too much is known about the two early Maidens, but in the next generation we come to Joe (1795–1864). Joe spent fifty-four years in Hunt Service and was undoubtedly a hard man. One day in 1829 when he was with the North Warwickshire, he slipped and fell into the huge copper in which water was being boiled up to prepare the hounds' food. His left leg was so badly scalded that the bone was exposed. Pause for a moment and consider that this accident happened in the days before antibiotics and analgesics. It is hardly surprising that 'many nights he could not close his eyes because of the agony of the limb . . .' The leg withered and shrivelled as it healed and became several inches shorter than the good leg.

By this time Joe was huntsman to the Cheshire, a post that he held for twelve years up until his retirement. In spite of his leg, he continued to hunt six days a week. Hunt six days a week and you are going to have falls. Joe's weakened leg kept breaking and he had to have several pieces of bone taken away from it (how are you feeling now?). In the end he got fed up with it and had it sawn off. Captain White, the Master of the Cheshire, wrote that he heard that Joe 'bore the operation like a man, which I was sure he would'. You might think that this would have ended Joe's career as huntsman. Not a bit: he had two wooden legs made – one for riding and one for walking and he continued hunting hounds until 1863.

Apart from being an interesting tale of fortitude, the story of Joe's hardships and his overcoming of them is relevant because it indicates the hardiness that can be said to be a part of the Maiden family make-up.

The dynasty continued. Joe's son Will (1849–71) and his son Will (1862–1934) both spent their lives in Hunt Service.

Jack's father (yet another Will) retired as Huntsman of the South Dorset in 1951.

Bert Maiden is Jack's younger brother. He reached the height of his powers as a famous huntsman of the Pytchley from 1960–71. At the age of sixty-two he is now Kennel Huntsman to the Eton College Beagles.

This brings us to Bert's son Chris, born in 1954. He is currently Huntsman to the Berkeley Hunt in Gloucestershire.

By my reckoning this makes eight generations who have successfully followed the same calling. I suspect that were you to have asked any of them why they have done what they have done, they would probably just say that they were 'bred to it'. As I said at the beginning: 'Blood will out.'

Chapter Sixty-Three

WINTER MORNING RITUAL

Frost: EVEN IN THE half light of dawn it is possible to see the white rime on the field outside the bedroom window. There is a skim of ice on the window, too. Shut the window at night? Heated bedrooms? Is it no wonder you have colds and sniffles.

Mind you, I do not spend long musing in front of the bedroom window during winter months. Several layers of clothing (layers are the secret) are assembled as soon as possible, even before an assault on the face with a cold water flannel. Brush the moustache and hair and that is the early morning toilette complete. Not very elaborate, perhaps, but good enough for rural and sub-zero Northumberland.

The Rayburn warm kitchen provides a welcome interlude for the pulling on of the extra socks and shepherding boots. Then comes the woollen cap, the sheepskin flying jacket and last, but not least, the mountain gloves.

The frozen hill air hits the face like a blow as I walk out of the door. The first blast of Northumbrian hill air reams out the lungs and makes them rasp and falter: it is the strongest air in Britain. There must have been a shower before the frost came and the concrete patch by the garage is a sheet of ice. I proceed with extreme caution, not wishing to 'cowp' (turn bustle over apex).

The collies come leaping and bouncing out of their kennels infected with the idiotic joy that frost brings to dogs. Their water buckets have become ice cubes and, of course, I forgot to put the hose in the shed last night and so it is a solid tube of ice. The ablution of the kennels will have to wait for later.

The four-wheeled motor bike (All Terrain Vehicle) has been safely tucked away in the warmth of the shed; even so it coughs and splutters a bit in protest at the cold — and cold it is, too. The frost seems to have sharpened as the light increases. I burrow a bit further into the high fleecy collar and think well of Mr Irvine who invented these splendid jackets.

I load the bag of feed and the bales of hay onto the little trailer behind the bike and set off down the drive, the dogs galloping and ragging each other. The sky is clear and white. The early sun is striking on the eastern face of the hills turning the bracken beds to pink. Hungry cows are blaring across the valley.

The track is a sheet of ice. I have to brake to avoid the tumbling collies. The ATV and trailer jackknife and we slide downhill sideways until the four-wheel drive finds something to bite on. I reason with the dogs in tones of christian charity.

The ewes have heard the engine and are waiting at the cattle grid, complaining loudly at the slackness of the service. The patches where they have lain through the night show black on the whitened grass.

A long line of cobs (large lumps of sheep cake) is spread out along the frosty ground. The greedy ewes dash up and down the line, desperate in case there is something better somewhere else. Some instincts run even deeper than hunger, however. In spite of the cold and the early hour, one of the tups chooses the moments of a ewe's preoccupation with food to have his way. You learn a lot about human nature from watching sheep.

It is nearly full light now. The colours on the hills change by the moment as the sun's rays strengthen and feel their way down the slope into darkened sykes and slacks. There is a covering of snow on the high tops: Hogden, Shilmoor and Hedgehope were all 'white ower'.

The water troughs are frozen. Pull the stick from its scabbard on the back of the ATV, break the ice, gloves off and take out the shards; otherwise, like a bone fracture, it will reseal twice as strong. The pursuit of slippery bits of ice in freezing water brings a glow to the hands. Gloves on.

Fill the hay hecks (racks) next. They are metal and the frost has frozen the lids down. Brute force is required. Now the gloves have to come off again to get out the knife and cut the strings as two bales are put in each rack. Here is a moment to savour; as each bale of well-made hay is opened, it releases on the cold winter air a momentary waft of the scents of summer.

My cheeks are burning as I chug into the yard but my nose wrinkles with pleasure. There is no better smell for a sharp-set man on a sharp bright morning than the scent of cooking bacon.

Chapter Sixty-Four

A MATCH
FOR LOVE, MONEY
OR MARBLES

THE FOXHOUND IS one of the most carefully bred animals in the world. Many foxhound pedigrees can be directly traced for more than two hundred years. Many brilliant minds have been brought to bear on the business of attempting to perfect this remarkable animal. Great minds do not always think alike. The foxhound and the breeding of it are matters that have produced a goodly boiling of controversy and bitter feelings.

In Britain there were (and are) differences of opinion over whether Welsh and Fell hound bloodlines should be allowed to mix with the racial 'purity' of the English Foxhound.

In the USA, the argument rages over the relative merits of the 'English' Foxhound and the 'Native American' Foxhound, which is only native in the sense that the various waves of settlers brought hounds with them over the years. The subject gets more complicated because there are something like fourteen different breeds of American Foxhound which have spin offs into Coon Hounds, Cross Breds and I do not know what all.

The English/American argument still continues but it reached its apogee of bitterness in 1905. There was a great deal of correspondence in the sporting press on the subject. The main protagonists were Harry Worcester Smith, Master of the Grafton Hunt in Massachusetts (American) and A. Henry Higginson, Master of the Middlesex Hunt, also in Massachusetts (English).

So savage did the controversy become that it was resolved

to hold a match in a 'fair hunting country': each competitor to bring hounds of his choosing and to hunt on alternate days 'for love, money or marbles'. Each adversary was to choose one judge and the two chosen judges were to appoint a third.

The match lasted eleven days and the Grafton won.

The fair hunting country chosen was that of the Piedmont Hunt in Virginia. There can be few fairer hunting countries in the world. The area is rather like parts of the Cotswolds. It is rolling pasture and pretty wooded creeks. There are beautifully kept farms around colonial mansions and the whole scene is set against the most pleasing background of the Blue Ridge Mountains. A fair country indeed and an ideal place to stage a modern match.

The 1989 match was between the Midland Hunt (Georgia) and the Piedmont. This put in contention two of the most formidable figures in foxhunting America: Mrs Archibald C. Randolph (aka 'Kingfish') Master of the Piedmont since 1954 and Benjamin H. Hardaway III, Master of the Midland since 1950, and who we have already met.

Mrs Randolph is now in her eighties and was not fit enough to attend, but her joint masters, Erskine L. Bedford and Randy M. Waterman — two flashing blades of old Virginia — were in charge.

Mr Hardaway is over seventy but is still 'big enough, rich enough and mean enough to have what I want' — and what he wants is the 'best pack of dawgs in America'.

The Midland Hounds are American July hounds crossbred with some of the best English lines.

The Piedmont are All American.

So the scene is set. Let us go hunting, but with one caution: 1905 was very much a grudge match and 1989 was to be a lot of fun amongst consenting sportsmen.

Day 1 — The Midland

The meet was in a field on 'George Chester's place', which is just off Route 17 in case you want to look on your map. A very large crowd and a mounted field of over seventy horses (invitation only) attended. The three eminent judges were Farnham F. Collins, Master of the Millbrook (NY); Dr Joe

Rogers, Master of the Loudoun Hunt (Va) and Bobby Joe Pillion, Whipper-in to the Blue Ridge (Va).

I got kissed by several lovely ladies which I find is a very good way to start the day. Mr Hardaway got kissed by Mrs Onassis which did not seem to be doing him any harm either. We then went hunting.

Mr Hardaway had given me his daughter, Mrs Page Flournoy, her broken collar bone and a portable radio to look after. We got in the pick-up driven by Mutt; Mutt has worked for Mrs Randolph for twenty-five years and is locally described as a 'real gennleman'. I cannot better that description.

This was the rough end of the Piedmont country, hard below the mountains, with rocky unkempt fields and steep, wooded bottoms. A difficult area to get around, the difficulty compounded by a railway line through the middle of it. All the hunt staff carry walkie-talkie radios on their saddles, a first rate idea.

It was a difficult day with minimal scent, but I thought that the Midland acquitted themselves well. The rules said that the judging would cease at three o'clock precisely, whatever hounds were doing. This was a pity, because at 1510 hounds found a big fox and had the best hunt of the day right up into the mountains, but the judges could take no account of it.

Mutt is a man of many parts. Apart from carrying one of the most comprehensively stocked mobile bars that it has been my pleasure to encounter, he also produced (with the flourish of a cloth) an amazing 'tailgate' picnic for everybody at the end of the day: all of it cooked by himself. He had been one of thirteen children and every child was expected to be able to do everything on the old home farm including cook. Mutt's ham biscuits are a memory that abide with me still.

Day 2 – The Piedmont's turn at Hastening Farm

The Piedmont have a much respected professional huntsman, Jimmy Atkins, who had his hounds in very fine fettle.

Once more Miz Flournoy, her collar bone and I were riding with Mutt. Once again there were plenty of foxes but very little scent.

We had a fine view of the first fox going away across open

country. There was a long check outside a graveyard and I had time to ponder on whether it was a handicap going through life having been christened Alphonson Johnson: he is past worrying about it now, anyway. It also gave Mr Hardaway (whom I had taken to calling 'Poppa') a chance to deliver a little moral lecture:

'Hear you behaved real sweet and clean yesterday: don't get drinkin' no likker now': as if I would.

The motorized followers got unsighted for a time but I (Big Daddy is my radio 'handle') was able to keep in radio contact with 'Fat Daddy' or, as it might be, Jesse Ford, the Midland Huntsman. From him we gleaned the news that they 'denned in some rocks', then they were 'trailin' up the crick'; 'they ain't doin' much', and 'they goin' to Miz Peck's'. Now you know as much about it as I did.

There were three foxes in a wood pile (Miz Peck's?) and we hunted one into the back gardens of Unison (pop. c.50) and that was really that.

Mutt had done the 'tailgate' again and the likker box received some serious attention from the followers.

That night it was Mr Hardaway's party at Welbourne which is a lovely colonial mansion in seventh-generation ownership of the same family. Nat and Sherry Morison face the same problems faced by many old families with old houses: they keep the problem at bay by running a very splendid Bed and Breakfast operation.

Americans are the most hospitable people and when they party, they party well. There is another thing that I like about the Americans: they like my singing. People in Britain will go to almost any lengths to prevent my bursting into song, but the Americans actually demand it.

'Hell, boy, this is my goddam party; now sing for your supper.' Who could resist such an invitation and so charmingly presented?

Day 3 – The Midland at Delaplane

This meet was on the edge of the best of the Piedmont Hunt country, which means some of the most lovely hunting country anywhere in the world. It was a day of bright sunshine with a bite in the air. A taut, tense sort of day: a day to make sure that your saddle girth was tight before you left the meet. The tension was heightened by the biggest mounted field so far, massed press photographers and rumours that the judges had the Piedmont leading by a nose.

The amazing Mutt knew exactly where to go, as always, so that we were in a good position to see the Midland hounds screaming away on their first fox, crossing the road just in front of us. We were also able to watch the mounted field jump in and out of the road, led by the dashing Mr Waterman. The back numbers were encouraged by Mutt's chant of: 'C'aint keep up, you better go home.'

Hounds disappeared into a deep valley and we had some furious driving round through Rectortown to keep in contention. Two foxes crossed the road in front of us, but they were obviously not being hunted.

Mutt managed to raise Johnny Klepper (the Piedmont Whipper-in) on his hand-set and was told to head for the Double Silos. ('Damned if Johnny ain't hard to hear when he's chewing baccer.') We found hounds marking to ground by the double silos, the mounted field steaming and heaving after what had been a very fast hunt.

Three foxes were soon afoot in the creek which echoed with the tremendous cry of the Midland hounds. All the foxes were greeted with much excited holloaing from the 'limo lock' on the valley road, in spite of Mutt's remonstrances. ('Miz Randolph would had two ears and a nose off each of 'em for holloaing.')

Then followed a period of continuous but more local hunting. This was mostly on land that belongs to the great Mr Paul Mellon where you become accustomed to the polite but careful scrutiny of large men in jeeps and bulky jackets.

'Wine Maker, Wine Maker: you eyeballed them? Kick it on back.' Mutt is on the CB radio.

'Sure thing, sure thing: they on by the air strip.'

'10–4' Down in to the valley again, to see hounds hunting along the cliff face. There were several dirty backs amongst the riders, denoting falls. Mutt chuckled and chortled. Everyone who falls has to donate a case of beer to the 'tailgate' bar.

Hounds eventually marked to ground in a drain under the drive of a house where a famous movie star had once lived. I asked someone whether she was indeed beautiful. He said that it all depended what time of the morning you saw her and make of that what you will.

It was getting late in the day now and although the competition had finished at 3 pm sharp, hunting continued. The steaming crowd, however, was gathered round Mutt's bar. Mr Hardaway took his hounds away from the hole and was calling loudly for beer because his mouth was like a —— then out popped the fox. Away went the hounds into the gathering dusk. There was a frantic ramming on of hats and scrambling back into saddles.

It was pitch black when hounds were finally collected and taken many miles back to where all the transport was. There was much shuttling of trailers and lorries in the dark before people got to enjoy the splendid Hunt Breakfast at the Plasketts' place.

I had scored the Midland at 9 out of 10 for the day and as I wished Mutt good night, he said, 'Them Piedmont dawgs goin' to have to do a mean bit of runnin' tomorrow.'

Day 4

Even the Welbourne breakfast (memorable) could not raise the mood on the next morning. The blizzard which was supposed to pass to the south, had turned north and was very definitely on the door step. Roads were blocked, airports closed.

Randy Waterman struggled in to drink some coffee with us. 'We're dead,' he said simply and the snowflakes thickened.

The result of the match was to have been announced at a dinner given by the Piedmont at Welbourne that night. For a time even the dinner seemed in jeopardy, but the Americans are accustomed to snow and over one hundred people sat down to dine that night.

It is probably fair to say after dinner commonsense temporarily evaporated. I mean, it cannot be regarded as commonsensible to be doing Texas Two Step at four o'clock in the morning. However I understand that the process is known in America as 'really hanging it out' and I am a great believer in adopting the customs of other countries.

So there it is. The Great Hunting Match of 1989 is still undecided. The last day is going to be held at some future date and the trophy will be awarded.

Who is going to win? That will be a matter for the judges, but I do not think it matters anyway. It was a great sporting occasion held in the best of sporting traditions. Above all, it was great fun; or, as the Americans would say 'a real blast'. I will go along with that.

Chapter Sixty-Five

A WALK AT
THE BACK END
OF THE YEAR

THE WINTER DOES NOT keep me out of the hills. In fact, I think the hills are at their best then, from the aesthetic point of view. The fat growth of summer has been stripped away by the frost and wind, leaving the hillsides clean and hard muscled. The rocks stand out black and sharp and the slopes are muted shades of brown and grey-green in the hard winter light, whilst the high tops are powdered with snow.

When time allows and my resident work ethic is having a nap, I take my bag and stick and go and climb a hill. Mind you, there are days when I am grateful to stay snug and warm at my desk. Days when I look out of the office window and see great hanging curtains of sleet coming across the valley. Days when the great storms come whooping and ranting out of the west and the rain is like a fist in the face. Days when the wind will rip a gate out of the hand and smash it to kindling. Days when the rain turns to ice on the coat. These are not good days for the hill.

Even on an apparently good day, the hills are never to be trusted or treated with contempt. The weather can change in a moment. Every 300 feet that you climb means a one degree drop in temperature, apart from any wind chill factor. Layers of clothing are the thing and plenty of them. Let the layers be wool, wool and more wool. Wool keeps you warm even when wet: ask any sheep.

In my bag I always carry a torch, an aluminium survival blanket (fits in a pocket), a whistle, a compass, a bar of chocolate and I *always* tell someone where I am going. There is a lot of hill out there; break a leg and you could take an awful lot of finding. I also take a flask of whisky that I may be merry in adversity.

One of my favourite routes starts with a 700-foot climb. It is my little conceit to do it without stopping. On the pinnacle of this particular hill is an old fort. It consists of two large drystone circles, one within the other and a ditch in between. The old camp has stunning views, but I do not suppose that that was the reason for building it there. It is in an extremely good defensive position with precipitous slopes on three sides.

Lack of wind is not a feature of this spot. Whatever the weather, there always seems to be a howling gale. I hate seeing my cap rolling briskly down the slope that I have just sweated up.

To the south of the fort is a wide, rolling, white grass plateau across which ambles an old green road. It is the same green road that I followed out of the valley. These old roads fascinate me: a person would be fairly dull of soul not to think of the millions of feet that have tramped the way before. At one time, this road would have been a busy thoroughfare. Only the shepherds and the sheep use it now.

It is good striding on the tops here, with the wind rustling the bents. The hills roll away on either side and there are glimpses of the river tumbling through the valley to the right. High above, a skein of geese heads south.

At the far side of the plateau is another fort: earth-walled this time and rectangular in shape. Again, it is well-sited defensively and it has one great advantage on the first one: access to water. A postern gate gives onto a steep little track that leads to a small burn and a reedy lake, from which there is usually an explosion of duck.

Northern winter days are short and the light is going by mid afternoon. There are already lights winking in the valley and the wind has a keener edge. A drift of scattered snowflakes makes one think of home. Another, gentler, green road leads back to the valley – to tea and, in view of the exercise that I have taken, a hot buttered crumpet.

INDEX